NOISES IN THE NIGHT!

Without doubt, Britain has the reputation of being the most haunted country in the world, one estimate putting its ghostly sites at ten thousand. Ghosts reflect the character and imagination of their race and times. Probe into the ghostlore of Cornwall, Wales and Scotland and what fantastical apparitions we encounter – so different from the conventional spectres of England.

Haunted Houses You May Visit gives details of eighty-eight sites where one can see White Ladies, headless horses, tragic lovers and so forth.

Also by Marc Alexander in Sphere Books:

THE DEVIL HUNTER

Haunted Houses You May Visit

MARC ALEXANDER

SPHERE BOOKS LIMITED
30-32 Gray's Inn Road, London WC1X 8JL

First published in Great Britain by Sphere Books Ltd 1982

For Noel and Kiri Hilliard

Printed and bound in Great Britain by
©ollins, Glasgow

CONTENTS

NUMBERS INDICATE PLACES
REFERRED TO IN
THE TEXT

ACKNOWLEDGEMENTS

The author wishes to express his sincere gratitude to the owners and curators of historic houses who gave up valuable time to provide information necessary for this book. He also wishes to thank The British Travel Association, The National Trust, the Bórd Fáilte Éireann, the British Library and the Colindale Newspaper Library for their helpful co-operation. Special thanks are due to Doreen Montgomery for her usual patience, to Barbara Boote for her skilful editing, Barbara Cheeseman for the preparation of the MS and finally to Simon Alexander for his map-reading.

Introduction

Haunted Houses.

What an evocative pair of words they are. As a child I found they instantly summoned up delightfully spooky visions of cobwebbed rooms, spindly forms glimpsed briefly at the end of corridors, skeletal fingers about to touch the back of your neck . . .

Sadly, as we get older we learn that there are more frightening things in real life than ghosts, yet for many of us they retain a fascination. What are they? Do they have a metaphysical significance? Do they even exist? Like UFOs and similar phenomena they have never been scientifically proved, yet a very large percentage of the population believes in them – or wants to believe in them. This is borne out by the fact that today stories about ghosts, whether factual or works of fiction, have never been so popular since Victorian times. Then 'spiritism' caught the popular imagination and its devotees felt they were on the threshold of a new spiritual dimension, not one that was only obtainable by blind faith but one that you could get in contact with through helpful spirit guides.

A century later we are in the same position as those Victorians. They had seen the structure of a nineteen-hundred-year-old faith eroded away in a few short years by Darwin's Theory of Evolution. The fundamentalist advocates who tried to halt it by scorn and dogma had no more chance of doing so than King Canute had of holding back the tide. With their organised belief crumbling about them, people needed a replacement – to many a psychic world that had little to do with religion seemed the answer.

Now our god called Science has failed us. In the early part of this century it seemed that Science was going to bestow upon us wealth, health and universal happiness. Disease, brutish labour, bad conditions, ignorance . . . all would be swept away and as brothers united by knowledge we would enter a brave new world. Since those halcyon days we have seen the world become a polluted place and the weapons provided by Science are a more terrible threat to Mankind than those for use against his natural

1

enemies. The old Jehovah may have been a jealous god, but Science has all the portents of being an annihilating one.

So, like our great-grandparents, we look for alternatives into which we can escape. We rediscover ley lines and look backward nostalgically to the pagan world, we try to find our way with computerised astrology, our young hit the trail to the ashram industry of the east . . . and many find an interest in the supernatural.

And so back to ghosts – and ghost stories.

Most of us hear of hauntings third or fourth hand.

'A friend of my cousin's stayed at this old place, somewhere down in Cornwall or was it Cumbria . . .' is a not uncommon opening. The aim of this book is to tell ghost stories and at the same time be a guide to the houses where they have taken place, and where you can actually walk up the haunted staircase or see a portrait of the Green Lady.

Without doubt, Britain has the reputation of being the most haunted country in the world, one estimate putting its ghostly sites at ten thousand, and there are good reasons why this island has such a large phantom population. Not having been conquered for the last nine centuries, nor having had an outside culture suddenly imposed upon it, it has preserved much of its folk traditions, including memories of hauntings.

I also believe the mingling of races has been responsible for an inherent awareness of psychical phenomena – the Beaker People who left behind such mysterious monuments, the Celts with their rainbow imaginations, the wyrd-ridden Saxons and the Normans with their austere spirituality.

Ghosts reflect the character and imagination of their race and times. Probe into the ghostlore of Cornwall, Wales and Scotland and what fantastical apparitions we encounter – so different from the conventional spectres of England. To me the most intriguing haunting ground is the borderlands of Cumbria and Northumberland where the wild apparitions of the Celt intermingle with the decorous 'radiant boys' and 'white ladies' of the Anglo-Norman.

Britain's haunted houses reflect this in the variety of hauntings which take place under their roofs. There are strong elemental forces, benign ghosts who revisit the scenes of their earthly happiness, bizarre manifestations such as spectral coaches drawn by headless horses, harbingers of death, tragic lovers and even household pets such as the little dog who returns to play at Ham House.

What is particularly interesting is the arbitrary interpretations placed upon paranormal phenomena suggesting that explanation, like beauty, is in the eye of the beholder. The Reformation, for example, was responsible for a plethora of nuns and monks who remained earthbound as a protest against the removal of the True Faith. Or so claimed the propagandists. The ghosts themselves never said.

In the course of researching and writing a number of books on the supernatural, the importance of stone has become more and more obvious to me. Our traditional haunted sites are old houses, castles and churches whose walls have stood for centuries, suggesting that there may be some quality in the material itself capable of retaining random paranormal emanations – rather as our modern recording techniques store sounds and images – which are 'replayed' at certain times, or when triggered by the presence of a psychic person.

Ghosts which appear in such settings nearly always belong to the cyclic variety, each 'performance' being a repetition of a previous one which gives the impression that the phantom is unaware of our material world in which he or she briefly appears. Such hauntings are completely different to those where, it would seem, the spirits of the dead consciously return to locations which hold nostalgia for them or to make contact with the living. Compared with the cyclic variety, the span of such hauntings is relatively short and they are not restricted to specific surroundings.

The hauntings dealt with in this book are mostly of the first category, being manifestations connected with particular sites and going through set routines.

It used to be a popular belief that such appearances were the result of some horrific experience, usually at the point of death, but this is not always so. While moments of high drama or of emotional intensity do get reproduced again and again through the ghostly videotape machine, so do inconsequential happenings.

Many hauntings appear to be without significance – such as a child walking down a path or sounds of footfalls on a stair – yet paradoxically it is this very mundaneness which strengthens my belief in the supernatural. I would be very suspicious if it conformed to human notions as it is our condition to see the world about us as 'through a glass, darkly'.

Although Britain has a great variety of haunted sites, it is the house which is of the most interest because its supernatural manifestations take place in everyday domestic situations. It is one thing to glimpse a phantom figure in a ruined castle, and quite another to wake up and find one in your bedroom. Thus haunted houses have always seized the popular imagination. In the thirties char-a-banc tours were organised for the curious to see Borley Rectory. A century ago England's most famous ghost site was No. 50 Berkeley Square. It was one of the things to do when visiting London to go to the square and stare at its grimed brick exterior . . . and shudder deliciously at the rumours whispered about its unearthly inhabitants. Although forgotten now, it was such a classic case that I think it is worth quoting the magazine *Mayfair* of 28 April 1879. 'It appears that the house had an evil reputation for being badly haunted so long ago as when it was last lived in . . . One day a maidservant, newly arrived, was put to sleep in one of the upper rooms. An hour or two after the household was at rest, it was awakened by fearful screams from the new servant's room and she was found staring in the middle of the floor, as rigid as a corpse, with hideously glaring eyes – she had suddenly become a hopeless and raving madwoman, but never found a lucid interval wherein to say what made her so. However, this, I would say, would not mean much, even when taken in connection with the character of the house and of the room – women may go mad now and then, without any ghostly dealings. The room was given up, but the house still remained occupied, and that seemed to be the end. But some little time afterwards a guest arrived when the house had many visitors; and he, not unnaturally, laughing at such a skeleton in the cupboard and perhaps, like many sceptics, inclined for a little experience in such ventures, eagerly volunteered for the room which all others were so shy of entering. It was arranged that if, after a certain time, he rang the bell for the room once, it was a sign that he felt himself as comfortable as could be expected; but that if he rung it twice, someone should come up and see what was the matter. At the end of the given time the bell only rang once, but presently the same bell gave a frantic peal; and those who ran to his aid found the ghost-defier a corpse. And dead men tell no tales.

'What had he or she seen, or felt, or heard, to kill the man on the spot, and send the woman out of her mind?'

The house's sinister reputation began at the end of the eighteenth century when a certain Mr Dupre was said to have confined his insane brother in one of the upstairs rooms. His violence was such that no one could handle him and he had to be fed through a special opening in the door. According to one legend it was the ghost of the maniac which became the Horror of Berkeley Square.

Other reports about the house suggested one of its ghosts was a child in a Scottish dress, who had been frightened to death by a sadistic servant in the nursery, another that there was the phantom of a girl who had thrown herself out of an upper-floor window to escape being raped by her uncle. Her ghost sometimes hovered outside the window, tapping on the panes of glass.

Lord Lyttelton spent a night in the haunted room and as a result wrote a famous short story 'The Haunters and the Haunted'. He armed himself with two guns loaded with silver coins. He survived the night though he fired at 'something' which came at him out of the darkness and which fell 'like a rocket' before disappearing.

During the 1870s, neighbours of the deserted house were alarmed by the sound of cries and the noise of heavy objects being dragged across bare boards, bells ringing and windows being slammed in true poltergeist fashion.

Towards the end of the last century another mystery was added to the story of No. 50 Berkeley Square. A journalist wrote: 'The house . . . is uninhabited, save by an elderly man and woman who act as caretakers; but even these have no access to the room. That is kept locked, and the key being in the hands of a mysterious and seemingly nameless person, he comes to the house once every six months, locks up the elderly couple in the basement, then unlocks the room and occupies himself in it for hours.'

Nearly a century has passed since No. 50 Berkeley Square enjoyed its ghastly reputation. Today it looks as respectable as its neighbours and is the office of a well-known firm of booksellers.

Few of the hauntings listed here are as melodramatic as that of No. 50 and I often got the impression that the resident ghost is regarded with affection rather than dread – almost as one of the family, which is true in some cases.

You will find that the accounts of hauntings in this book vary in length from a couple of paragraphs to several pages. This is in ratio to what is known about the phenomena. Not all haunted stately homes have the dramatic ingredients of Glamis Castle or Sandford Orcas Manor – sometimes it is an unknown phantom who appears briefly for an unknown reason, and about which very little can be said.

What may come as a surprise is the small number of Irish hauntings. This is not because Ireland is short of ghosts, but because there are relatively few houses open to the public. The Irish Tourist Board lists thirty whereas in England alone there are over 850.

Visiting Haunted Houses

The haunted houses described in this book are all in the category of stately homes or houses of historic interest, and as such may be visited by the public. Some are recipients of grants from the Historic Buildings Council in return for which their owners must open for a few days each year or allow people to visit them by appointment. This is preferably arranged by letter and relevant details are provided with such entries.

Periods when the houses are open are given but as times of entry can be altered it is best to check before your visit. This can be done by telephoning the house or by buying a publication containing up-to-date information, such as the annual *Historic Houses, Castles and Gardens* which not only lists opening times but location, cost of entry and other helpful information.

Houses in the care of the Department of the Environment have Standard Hours of opening which are:–

16 October to 14 March, weekdays 9.30 hrs to 16.00 hrs,
Sunday 14.00 hrs to 16.00 hrs.
15 March to 15 October, weekdays 9.30 hrs to 18.30 hrs,
Sunday 14.00 hrs to 18.30 hrs.

In some cases properties are also open on Sunday mornings from 9.30 hrs from April to September.

ENGLAND

Bedfordshire

WOBURN ABBEY
(Map reference: 87)

This entertainment complex is at Woburn, five miles from Exit 12 or 13 on the M1 Motorway. It has been the home of the Dukes of Bedford for over three centuries and with it the present duke pioneered the stately home business in Britain when he opened its doors to the public in 1955. Since then literally millions of people have inspected its treasures and enjoyed its unique antiques shopping market, Wildlife Centre and 3000-acre deerpark.

In the mid-18th century the house was rebuilt by Inigo Jones and Henry Flitcroft, and further additions were made by Henry Holland early next century.

Today Woburn has what is considered to be one of the most important private art collections in the world which includes works by Canaletto, Cuyp, Rembrandt, Reynolds, Teniers, Velasquez and others. There are also etchings by Queen Victoria. Other delights include collections of English and French furniture from the 18th century, silverware and the magnificent Sèvres dinner service presented by Louis XV of France to the fourth Duke of Bedford.

> *Opening times:* Daily throughout the year except on Christmas Day and the four days preceding it. The times of visiting vary, the house and park having different admission times but both are open in the afternoons from 1 January to Easter and 1 November to 31 December, with morning opening from Good Friday to 31 October.
> *Telephone:* Woburn 666.

The idea of this book came some years ago when His Grace, the thirteenth Duke of Bedford, told me about the curious haunting of Woburn Abbey. This extraordinary man, who so blatantly pioneered the stately home industry which brings pleasure to millions and ensures that the nation's treasured houses are properly preserved, quite casually triggered an interest which developed as I learned of more and more haunted houses open to the public.

'The ghost became such a nuisance that we had to change our television room,' the duke said. 'We'd be sitting there when suddenly the handle of the door at one end of the room would turn and the door would open just as though an invisible person was coming through.'

A few seconds later, in the time it would take for a person to walk the length of the room, the handle of the door at the opposite end would turn again as though held by an invisible hand. It seems that after the family gave up using the room for viewing the ghost moved its door-opening activity to a couple of bedrooms, sometimes the phenomenon occurring several times during the night, to the annoyance of the occupants.

An explanation for the unseen entity was that he was a young man who in the past was horribly ill-treated at the abbey, being partially strangled before being thrown out of a window, dragged to one of the lakes on the estate and drowned. But why this unfortunate should return to the house to open doors is a complete mystery.

The other ghost to haunt the house is a figure in a brown habit who has been seen on many occasions in the crypt. He probably goes back to Tudor times when, just before the Dissolution, the abbot of Woburn was hanged from an oak which still stands in the grounds for his opposition to Henry VIII's marriage to Anne Boleyn.

The other haunted spot the duke mentioned is a small summerhouse which is the only place to be barred to visitors on the estate. To understand the sad atmosphere which surrounds it we must look briefly at the life of the duke's grandmother who became known to the public as the Flying Duchess. As anyone who has read the duke's autobiography *A Silver Plated Spoon* will know, his grandfather, the eleventh duke, was a remote and implacable man. Having met his wife in India, he brought her to England where his parents did their best to make her feel unwelcome. Her unhappiness over this continued when she went to live as duchess in Woburn in 1891, her husband refusing her any say over the upbringing of their son or in the management of the cold, unhappy place which was her new home.

The new duchess was a lady of great spirit and she refused to be reduced to a nonentity. The duke might play the role of the heavy

Victorian husband, but he could not prevent her having a life of her own. The duchess caused a ripple of disapproval throughout aristocratic circles when the rumour spread that she had enrolled as a trainee nurse. With characteristic determination she qualified in the new field of radiography and as a theatre sister and then opened a model cottage hospital at Woburn, assisting with the operations and doing all the radiographic work.

Her other interests lay in ornithology and flying. She received her nickname in 1930 when, at the age of 64, she and a co-pilot made a record-breaking flight to South Africa in the course of which a forced landing was made in the jungle when the aircraft caught fire.

Despite these outlets, the duchess's unhappiness continued, especially when her husband declared that the upkeep of her hospital was too much and closed it down. From then on she spent most of her time sitting in the solitude of her summerhouse, watching the birds who regarded it as a sanctuary. Then on 22 March 1937 she announced that she was going to take up her Gypsy aeroplane for a flight so she would be able to log her two-hundredth hour of solo flying time. She taxied up a field, climbed into the sky over Woburn and was never seen again.

According to her flight plan her course was inland, yet six days after she disappeared her wrecked Gypsy was washed up on an east coast beach.

Although the present duke had a room set up in the abbey devoted to the memory of his grandmother, he believes that it is to the lonely little summerhouse that her spirit returns.

'Every time I come here I feel her very strongly,' he has said, and it seems that it is not only her personality which is apparent but a sense of the unhappiness which surrounded so much of her life.

Berkshire

WINDSOR CASTLE
(Map reference: 86)

Standing close to the River Thames twenty-one miles from London Windsor Castle, covering over twelve acres, is the largest inhabited castle in the world. It is one of Britain's main royal residences and the headquarters for the Order of the Garter. William the Conqueror built a fortress on this site at the same time he was building the Tower of London though, unlike the Tower, none of that original construction remains. Henry II replaced William's work with stone buildings, and he was followed in expanding the castle by Henry III, Edward III, Edward IV and Henry VIII while Charles II was responsible for the state apartments. The castle owes its present story-book appearance to George IV who commissioned the architect Jeffry Wyatville to improve it.

Treasures of historical interest fill the state apartments, including collections of armour, period furniture and paintings, especially works by Van Dyck. Of particular interest to many visitors is Queen Mary's Dolls' House which was designed by Sir Edwin Lutyens and presented to the queen in 1923.

Opening times: The castle is subject to closure at short notice for obvious reasons, but normally the precincts are open daily except for 15 June. The castle itself is open daily, excluding Sundays, though from late October to the middle of March the closing time is mid-afternoon. As the state apartments and Queen Mary's Dolls' House are closed at certain times it is best to check first if you particularly want to see them.
Telephone: Windsor 68286.

Windsor Castle is reputed to be haunted by four royal ghosts. Taking them in chronological order, they are Henry VIII, Queen Elizabeth I, Charles I and George III. The spirit of Henry VIII manifests itself aurally, being a sound of weary footsteps as the monarch – who grew gross and dropsical towards the end of his life – drags himself painfully along a corridor. A sound of wheezing breath underlines his struggle, and the pain he suffered from the ghastly ulcer in his leg. Alas that the body of the splendid young sportsman, whom the English had welcomed as bluff Prince Hal, should have run to this indulged flesh and thus be perpetuated through some psychic process.

In February 1897 Carr Glynn, a lieutenant in the Grenadier Guards, was reading in one of the rooms of the Queen's Library when he saw a lady, dressed in black and wearing a lace scarf of the same colour over her hair and shoulders, walk out of an inner room and cross the chamber. He heard the sound of her shoes on the polished wood floor and could have almost touched her as she walked past him and disappeared into a corner.

At first Lieutenant Glynn thought she must have gone through a doorway into another room. A moment later one of the castle servants entered the reading room and the lieutenant questioned him as to the identity of the dark lady. The man replied emphatically that nobody had entered the room.

Greatly mystified, Lieutenant Glynn rose and went to the room into which he had seen the lady disappear. It was empty and there was no exit by which she could have left!

The attendant then told him hesitantly that he must have glimpsed the ghost of Queen Elizabeth. She had been seen before, walking across the library in exactly the same way as the Guards officer described.

Charles I is said to revisit the Canon's House which stands in the castle's grounds. Although many ghosts of those who were beheaded are said to appear in their decapitated state, the shade of the tragic king is complete, the face being remarkably like the melancholy features depicted in his famous portraits.

The reign of George III was marred by the monarch's bouts of insanity although this did nothing to diminish the affection that many of his subjects felt for him. They nicknamed him 'Farmer George' because of his intense interest in horticultural matters; his popularity can be gauged by the universal delight – and the monuments – which celebrated his returns to sanity. But the last decade of his life – from 1810, when the Prince of Wales was appointed Regent, until 1820 – the king was in a state of permanent mental derangement, passing his days in a room at

Windsor playing on his harp. Now his spectre returns to the apartments where he was restrained.

Apart from royal ghosts, the most illustrious spirit to have manifested itself in Windsor Castle is that of Sir George Villiers, the father of the ambitious Duke of Buckingham who, as 'Steenie' the pampered favourite of James I, became the wealthiest and most influential man in the kingdom. After the death of James, Buckingham retained his position of power through his friendship with Charles I, having negotiated the king's marriage with Henrietta Maria of France. As he continued to hold the same power over the son as he had the father, he became one of the most hated men in England.

Edward Hyde, the first Earl of Clarendon, wrote in his *History of the Rebellion in England*, published in 1707, that Buckingham was so unpopular that prophecies and predictions of his death became current. No doubt these were merely forms of wishful thinking, but Clarendon wrote: 'Among the rest there was one which was upon a better foundation of credit than usually such stories are founded upon. In February 1628 an officer at Windsor Castle woke one night to see a man of very venerable aspect, who drew the curtains of his bed, and, fixing his eyes upon him, asked if he knew him.'

The startled officer did not reply at first, but at length managed to mutter that the midnight visitor resembled Sir George Villiers.

The ghost replied that he was right and said that he wanted him to perform an errand. He should go to the Duke of Buckingham and warn him that 'if he did not somewhat ingratiate himself to the people, or at least abate the extreme malice they had against him, he would be suffered to live but a short time'.

Then the phantom faded away and the officer, thinking he had been the victim of a nightmare, drifted back into sleep.

The next night the ghost reappeared, and again asked the officer to go to his son with the message. Still the officer ignored the request, believing in the reassurance of the morning light that he was the subject of a recurring dream.

On the third night Sir George manifested yet again, charging him to warn the duke. The officer, now accustomed to these night visitations, answered that it would be difficult to get the duke to take notice of such a wild tale, whereupon the ghost confided in him 'two or three particulars' which he said he must not mention to anybody but the duke.

13

Impressed at last that he had seen a real spectre, the officer rode to London the next day and managed to get himself admitted into the Buckingham household where he was conducted to the duke by Sir Ralph Freeman.

Afterwards the officer told Sir Ralph that when he mentioned 'those particulars which were to gain him credit', Buckingham went white and swore that the information was known only to himself and one other person.

Having listened to the warning, the duke went hunting with Charles I, but it was obvious to the rest of the party that his heart was not in it and very soon he left the field. He rode to his mother's house where he stayed with her for three hours, talking so excitedly that the sound of their voices came through the wall of the room where they were closeted.

Clarendon wrote that when Buckingham left his mother 'his countenance appeared full of trouble, with a mixture of anger, a countenance that was never before observed in him in any conversation with her, towards whom he had a profound reverence'.

On 23 August of that year the Duke of Buckingham was assassinated at Portsmouth by a discontented subaltern named John Felton who became a popular hero overnight.

Clarendon concluded: 'Whatever there was of all this it is a notorious truth that when the news of the Duke's murder was made known to his mother, she seemed not in the least surprised, but received it as if she had foreseen it, nor did afterwards express such a degree of sorrow as was expected from such a mother for the loss of such a son.'

In the long walk of the Great Park, belonging to Windsor Castle, a Grenadier Guard recruit committed suicide while on sentry duty. A few weeks later a soldier doing the same spell of duty saw the shadowy form of the young suicide in the moonlight. But a much more spectacular phenomenon which has been witnessed in the Great Park is the Wild Hunt led by Herne the Hunter, immortalised in Harrison Ainsworth's *Windsor Castle*.

In this book Herne is described as the Foul Field of the Forest, but students of mythology would recognise the wild figure with antlers growing from its head as a survivor from pagan times when dressing up as beasts was part of seasonal ritual.

The better-known legend of Herne dates back to the reign of

Richard II when Herne was a keeper in the royal forest. One day the king was hunting when a wounded stag turned upon him, and he would have suffered great injury had not the keeper leapt upon the animal and slaughtered it with his knife, although he was badly gored in doing so. When his body was pulled away from that of the dead stag it was seen that he was dying.

At that moment a stranger walked out of the trees and told the king that if he agreed to his form of magical treatment he could save the servant's life. Richard gave his assent and the man removed the stag's antlers and bandaged them to Herne's head, after which he asked that Herne be carried on a litter to his hut where he would nurse him until he recovered.

As Herne was borne away the king told him that when he was well again he would be appointed head huntsman. This created jealousy among the rest of the hunters. By the time they reached the stranger's hut they were determined that the order of promotion should not be upset by Herne and they made it clear to the wizard that if he wanted to save his life he would see to it that Herne did not recover.

The wizard replied that Herne was under his guardianship and he could not harm him, but if the huntsmen dared to suffer Herne's curse he would see to it that Herne did not remain the hunt leader for long. The men laughed off the idea of a curse and were delighted to see that when Herne returned he seemed to suffer from amnesia as far as the Great Park was concerned.

It was as though he had forgotten the geography of the forest and the tracks along which the deer ran, and each hunt he led was doomed to failure. After several disappointing days of sport, the king lost his temper and dismissed Herne. Embittered by the disgrace, Herne committed suicide that night. He hanged himself from the branch of a huge oak tree which, until 1863 when it was blown down during a gale, was known as Herne's Oak.

One of the hunters who had threatened the wizard to bring about Herne's downfall was walking through a grove when he saw the body swinging in the wind. He rushed to tell his companions but when they returned there was no trace of the body. Perhaps the man was mocked for drunken imaginings, but from then on the misfortune which had befallen Herne befell the huntsmen, and soon the king was so annoyed with their ineptitude that they realised they too were in danger of dismissal. They went to the hut in the forest and consulted the wizard who explained that until they had made some atonement to the earth-bound spirit of Herne they would have no luck.

Following his instruction they congregated about the old tree at midnight, whereupon the phantom of Herne – with antlers growing from his head – appeared and, leaping on to an equally ghostly horse, commanded them to follow him through the forest. Through the night the wild hunt, led by the spectral hunter, combed the forest for deer, and it was so successful that when the king went hunting there was not an animal left for his sport.

Realising there was something uncanny about the disappearance of game, he forced the story from one of the hunters. That night he went to Herne's Oak. Herne duly materialised at midnight and promised the king if the huntsmen who had betrayed him were punished he would cease to haunt the wood as long as the king reigned. Richard agreed and next morning ordered the conspirators to be hanged, after which he had no more trouble in finding game in Windsor park. But after his murder in 1400 the ghost of Herne the Hunter was seen again in the Great Park.

Queen Victoria ordered that a new tree was to be planted where Herne's Oak had been uprooted, and it was said that whenever the nation faced troubled times the ghost of the hunter would appear there. A story circulated that he had materialised just before the abdication of Edward VIII in 1936.

Buckinghamshire

CHENIES MANOR HOUSE
(Map reference: 20)

Built in the delightful village of Chenies close to the junction of the
A404 and the B485, the manor until recently belonged to the
Dukes of Bedford. Their ancestor John Russell acquired the place
in 1530 so that he could offer its hospitality to Henry VIII and his
courtiers. His wives Catherine Howard and Anne Boleyn also
stayed there. Other royal visitors included that indefatigable
houseguest Elizabeth I.

Apart from secret hiding places and passages, the house boasts
an ancient well and a garden. Among its objects of interest is a
collection of antique dolls.

> *Opening times:* Wednesday and Thursday afternoons from
> the first week of April to the end of October, also Spring and
> Summer Bank Holiday Monday afternoons.
> *Telephone:* Little Chalfont 2888.

Chenies Manor has the distinction of having once had Charles I
as a guest though it was no royal occasion. The sad monarch was
a prisoner of the Parliamentarians, and perhaps it is his heavy
footsteps which have echoed down the centuries, and which are
said to make the floorboards actually creak. This aural manifestation takes place close to a room where Queen Elizabeth I
once slept.

CLAYDON HOUSE
(Map reference: 22)

To be found at Middle Claydon, thirteen miles north-west of
Aylesbury, the house is a monument to the work of Lord Verney's
carpenter, Luke Lightfoot, who declared he would make it 'such a
Work as the World never saw'. The decorations in the main
downstair rooms particularly underline his skill. The house was

begun by Lord Verney in 1768 but he was bankrupted fifteen years later, and many of Claydon's contents had to be sold off. Perhaps the most remarkable feature of the house is its magnificent parquetry and wrought iron staircase whose balustrade is so finely made that its ornamental corn stalks are said to rustle when someone passes them.

Florence Nightingale often stayed at the house and today visitors can see her bedroom as well as mementos such as some of her letters and an orange she gave to a wounded soldier in the Crimea.

The Verney family still live in part of the house which is in the care of The National Trust.

> *Opening times:* Afternoons, excepting Thursday and Friday, from April to the end of October.
> *Telephone:* Steeple Claydon 349.

It is the spectre of Sir Edmund Verney which returns to Claydon House – and for a very bizarre reason. Sir Edmund had died for the king at the Battle of Edgehill in 1642. It had been his honour to be the Royal Standard-bearer, and so dedicated was he to his duty that when Parliamentarian troops captured him, he shouted 'My life's my own, my standard is the king's!' At this the Roundheads killed him but his hold on the standard pole was so strong that they were unable to wrest it from his hand.

The banner was soon recaptured and to their amazement the cavaliers found that the staff was still gripped by a severed hand, a hand they recognised as Sir Edmund's by a signet ring on one of the fingers.

His body was never recovered at the scene of the battle, but his hand was brought with full honour and interred at Claydon, and it is believed that it is this relic which is the focal point of the knight's manifestations. He appears close to the Red Stairs with a severed wrist, and the traditional explanation for his visits is that he is searching for his hand.

Another Claydon ghost has been seen in the Rose Room, and it has been suggested that this grey female figure could be the spectre of Florence Nightingale who stayed at the house after her sister had married into the Verney family.

Cheshire

CAPESTHORNE HALL
(Map reference: 16)

This Jacobean-style house stands off the A34 seven miles south of Wilmslow, close to the Jodrell Bank radio telescope. Here the Bromley-Davenport family has lived since the time of the Domesday book. The present house dates from the 18th century and recent research found that it was the work of the architects Francis and William Smith. It was renovated by Edward Blore in 1837 and again by the famous Anthony Salvin twenty-four years later.

Today the hall is noted for its magnificent staircase and a beautiful little Georgian chapel adjoining it.

> *Opening times:* Sunday afternoons from 29 March to 27 September, Wednesday and Saturday afternoons from May to September, and Tuesday and Thursday afternoons from July to September, also Bank Holiday Mondays and Good Friday.
> *Telephone:* Chelford 861221.

A few years ago the butler of Capesthorne told the Press that the resident ghost in the house had been seen so frequently that there could be no doubt about his authenticity, and he described her as 'a lady in a greyish dress'. A Member of Parliament, Sir Charles Taylor, was in the west wing when he saw the grey lady glide past him as he was about to go up a flight of stairs.

Apart from this rather traditional phantom other paranormal manifestations have been experienced at Capesthorne, one of which had more than a hint of horror about it. A number of 'spectre-like' shapes were once seen descending the steps into the chapel vault – perhaps that was less frightening than if they had been seen coming out!

What was really unpleasant was an occurrence in 1958 when a member of the family was roused from his sleep by a frantic rapping at his bedroom window. He opened his eyes to see an arm on the other side of the pane whose hand was apparently trying to find a way in.

As the window was ten metres above the ground it seemed that the intruder could only be on a ladder. The young man climbed out of bed and rushed to the window, doubtless expecting to be faced by a burglar. To his horror the arm vanished as he reached the window, and in the moonlight he saw that there was no ladder propped against the wall – and the courtyard below was deserted.

GAWSWORTH HALL
(Map reference: 36)

The hall at Gawsworth, near Macclesfield, is a half-timbered 16th-century manor house in a perfect setting. Historically it is interesting as the home of Mary Fitton who was Maid of Honour to Elizabeth I. Today its attractions include a carriage museum.

Opening times: Afternoons from 21 March to 25 October.
Telephone: North Rode 456.

Down the centuries various forms of paranormal phenomena have been experienced at Gawsworth Hall, usually without much comment from the owners because such things seem so in keeping with a house that goes back so far into history. One of the most recent manifestations – in 1971 – was the aroma of incense which permeated the air close to a small secret room in which priests had been hidden in the days of Catholic persecution.

The main Gawsworth ghost is that of 'a lady in ancient costume', and it is thought she might be Mary Fitton who earned the wrath of Queen Elizabeth. Mary was the daughter of Sir Edward Fitton, who inherited Gawsworth from his father in 1579, and who used his influence at court to get her appointed as a Maid of Honour.

Mary must have been a striking young woman as it was rumoured she was the Dark Lady of Shakespeare's sonnets. But sometimes at court it paid not to be too beautiful. When she had been in the queen's service for six years Sir Robert Cecil – who presumably kept an eye on such matters – reported to Her

Majesty that she was pregnant. The fury of the Virgin Queen was awesome – perhaps she was jealous of her Maid, having referred to herself as 'a barren stock' – and as a punishment for her 'effrontery' Mary was imprisoned in the Tower of London. With her went the Earl of Pembroke for the part he played in the 'effrontery'.

Whether Mary Fitton was the Dark Lady of the sonnets, whether it is her phantom which glides about Gawsworth Hall, are matters for conjecture but with such a background she certainly seems *right* to be the ghostly inhabitant of such a magnificent medieval house.

LYME PARK
(Map reference: 58)

Half a mile west of Disley on the A6 is Lyme Park which dates from Elizabethan times and an earlier building which stood on the site is referred to in a manuscript written in 1465. The house got its present appearance in 1720 when Giacomo Leoni was commissioned to redesign its appearance and gave it a Palladian exterior. Having been the home of the Legh family for six centuries one can expect interesting period furnishings, while attractions outside in the 1320-acre park include formal gardens, a nature trail and a herd of red deer. The estate is now in the care of The National Trust who lease it to the Stockport and Greater Manchester Councils.

Opening times: Afternoons daily, excluding Mondays, apart from Bank Holidays, from April to October.
Telephone: Disley 2023.

The haunting of Lyme Park recalls a romance which ended in despair and death. In 1422 Sir Piers Legh, a knight who followed Henry V in his French campaign, died in Paris with a last request that his body should be buried in the estate which he loved. Later, as the cortège slowly approached the Park, black-clad members of the household went forward to meet it. Among them was Lady Blanche who had been desperately in love with the dead knight.

Seeing his coffin return instead of him riding gaily at the head of his men was too much for the girl. The shock killed her and since then her mourning ghost has been seen in the Long Gallery. But this is not the only paranormal reminder of that tragic home-coming – in the grounds a spectral funeral procession sometimes reappears and moves slowly towards the house before fading away.

Cornwall

GODOLPHIN HOUSE
(Map reference: 38)

This former residence of the Earls of Godolphin is to be found near the village of Godolphin Cross five miles north-west of Helston. Parts of the house go back to Tudor times, with additions made in Elizabethan and Caroleon periods. Most interesting from an architectural viewpoint is the front resting on columns of local granite which was built just before the Civil War.

Opening times: Thursday afternoons in May and June, and Tuesday and Thursday afternoons from July to the end of September.
Telephone: Germoe 2409.

Like Glamis Castle, Godolphin House has its mysteries built into it. Few of us can resist being intrigued by the idea of a secret passage, and here it is said there are five to whet our curiosity. They are believed to have been designed as escape routes to ensure the safety of Charles II, but it is in connection with Godolphin's sealed closet that the house's supernatural reputation is based. From this mysterious room a glimmering phantom – a traditional White Lady – has been seen to emerge and then glide along the terrace on some long unknown errand.

Cumbria

CORBY CASTLE
(Map reference: 24)

Close to Great Corby on the east bank of the appropriately called Eden, this mansion stands in extensive grounds overlooking the lively river and its well-wooded banks. It was originally a 13th-century pele tower owned by the Vaux and Richmond families before coming into the possession of Andrew Harcla, the Earl of Carlisle, who was executed for treason in 1322. Subsequently it was taken over by the Salkeld family and then, in the 17th century, by the Howards. In the 19th century they gave it the elegant appearance it has today by adding a three-storey porticoed hall.

> *Opening times:* Daily, 1 April to 31 October.
> *Telephone:* Wetheral 60246.

Corby Castle is mentioned in almost every book on English hauntings, perhaps because Mrs Catherine Crowe told such a fascinating story of its ghost in her classic two-volume work *The Night Side of Nature* which was published in 1848.

The 19th-century additions must have been still fairly new when Mrs Crowe visited Corby, where she copied out an account of the 'Radiant Boy', who appeared occasionally in one of the castle chambers, from a journal kept by a member of the family. Dated 3 September 1803, the writer explained that among the guests who had visited the castle was the Rector of Greystoke and his wife.

> According to previous arrangements, they were to have remained with us some days, but their visit was cut short in a very unexpected manner. On the morning after their arrival we were all assembled at breakfast, when a chaise-and-four dashed up to the door in such haste that it knocked down part of the fence of my flower-garden. Our curiosity was, of course, awakened to know who could be arriving at so early an hour,

when, happening to turn my eyes towards Mr A—, I observed that he appeared extremely agitated.

'It is our carriage,' said he. 'I am very sorry, but we absolutely must leave you this morning.'

We naturally felt, and expressed, considerable surprise, as well as regret, at this unexpected departure, representing that we had invited Colonel and Mrs S—, some friends whom Mr A— particularly desired to meet, to dine with us on that day. Our expostulations, however, were in vain; the breakfast was no sooner over than they departed, leaving us in consternation to conjecture what could possibly have occasioned so sudden an alteration in their arrangements. I really felt quite uneasy lest anything should have given them offence; and we reviewed all the occurrences of the preceding evening, in order to discover, if offence there was, whence it had arisen. But our pains were in vain; and after talking a great deal about it for some days, other circumstances banished the matter from our minds.

It was not till we some time afterwards visited the part of the county in which Mr A— resides that we learnt the real cause of his sudden departure from Corby. The relation of the fact, as it here follows, is in his own words:

'Soon after we went to bed we fell asleep. It might be between one and two in the morning when I awoke. I observed that the fire was totally extinguished; but although that was the case, and we had no light, I saw a glimmer in the middle of the room, which suddenly increased to a bright flame. I looked out, apprehending that something had caught fire; when, to my amazement, I beheld a beautiful boy clothed in white, with bright locks, resembling gold, standing by my bedside, in which position he remained some minutes, fixing his eyes upon me with a mild and benevolent expression. He then glided gently towards the side of the chimney, where it is obvious there is no possible egress, and entirely disappeared. I found myself again in total darkness, and all remained quiet until the usual hour of rising. I declare this to be a true account of what I saw at Corby Castle, upon my word as a clergyman.'

In her book Mrs Crowe commented that she was acquainted with some of the family and several of the friends of the clergyman, adding:

I can positively assert that his own conviction with regard to the nature of this appearance has remained ever unshaken. The circumstances made a lasting impression upon his mind, and he never willingly speaks of it; but when he does, it is always with the greatest seriousness, and he never shrinks from avowing his belief that what he saw admits of no other interpretation than the one he then put upon it.

According to tradition the appearance of the Radiant Boy heralds a rise to fame and fortune – followed by a violent end – for the beholder, though this does not appear to have befallen the Rector of Greystoke. A well-known story is that a similar Radiant Boy appeared to a Captain Robert Stewart in northern Ireland who afterwards became Lord Castlereagh, the great Foreign Secretary who 'became the soul of the coalition against Napoleon' but later, in 1822, committed suicide with a penknife.

DACRE CASTLE
(Map reference: 28)

A few miles north-west of Lowther, across the River Eamont, which flows from Ullswater, the castle stands by Dacre village. It consists of a keep with four corner turrets, and is a cross between a Border pele tower and a proper castle. Built in the 14th century, the roof was replaced in the 17th and apart from that it has hardly been altered.

Visiting only by written appointment.

A puzzling haunting with a touch of ancient royalty is still reported from time to time at Dacre Castle.

King Athelstan had given his sister in marriage to Sithric, King of Northumbria, but the latter failed to meet his obligations to the Saxon monarch. He died before retribution could catch up with him, but his two sons, Anlaf and Guthred, were forced to flee to the court of King Constantine of Scotland who attempted to regain Northumbria for the brothers with the aid of King Donal of Strathclyde. Their campaign failed and finally the two northern kings met Athelstan to hear his terms at the site of Dacre Castle.

The meeting was barely over when the kingdoms of the North decided to humble the Saxon king, and to this end they were joined by the Kings of Cumbria, Wales, Ireland, and a fleet of over 600 Danish ships which sailed into the Humber and occupied Northumbria.

It seemed the Saxons would be overwhelmed by the confederation of Celts and Danes which faced them on the field of Brunnanburgh, but, led by King Athelstan and his brother Edmund, they attacked with such valour that they won the day. A poem in the *Anglo-Saxon Chronicle* described their victory in words giving us a taste of the enthusiasm for war which was the keynote of the Dark Ages.

'Then the Norsemen departed in their nailed ships,' the unknown poet wrote, 'bloodstained survivors of spears, on Dingesmere over the deep water to seek Dublin, Ireland once more, sorry of heart. The two brothers likewise, king and atheling both, sought their own country, the land of the West Saxons, exulting in war. They left behind them, to joy in the carrion, the black and horn-beaked raven with his dusky plumage, and the dun-feathered eagle with his white-tipped tail, greedy hawk of battle, to take toll of the corpses . . .'

Why the shades of the three kings who met before this bloody conflict should continue to return to Dacre Castle none can say, but – though many centuries have passed since the ravens fed on their dead followers – their spectres still appear in the grounds about the castle from time to time.

LEVENS HALL
(Map reference: 55)

Five miles south of Kendal on the A6 is this fine Elizabethan house which began as a North Country pele tower. The tower is to the right of the entrance, but it was eclipsed by the building which was undertaken in 1580 by the Bellinghams. Their decoration of the rooms is still to be seen, and Levens is well known for its magnificent plasterwork as well as its collection of furniture. The topiary gardens, designed by Monseigneur Beaumont at the end of the 17th century, have hardly changed since his day and are as famous as the house.

Opening times: Tuesday, Wednesday, Thursday, Sunday afternoon, and Bank Holiday Monday afternoons from

Easter Sunday to 30 September. The gardens open in the morning each day.

Telephone: Sedgwick 60321.

There are several ghosts at Levens; a pink lady who appears only when children are present, a small black dog which materialises so close to visitors' feet that they try to step over it, and the Grey Lady who, in the coaching days, was responsible for near accidents by appearing suddenly before the horses. She carries on the tradition today by materialising in front of cars as they go up the driveway to the hall, causing drivers to slam on their brakes in the fear that they are about to run down an old lady. By the time they have wound down their windows to give her some advice on road usage, they find that she has melted away. One of the Bagot family, the owners of the Hall, once cycled straight through her. She is the most interesting ghost at Levens as she is said to have been an old gypsy woman who cursed the family living there.

The story goes that long ago she turned up at the Hall begging for bread, but was turned away by a hard-hearted owner. She died of starvation soon afterwards, but just before she died she declared that 'no son will inherit the house until the River Kent ceases to flow and the white fawn is born'. Strangely the inheritance of Levens Hall has gone from relative to relative rather than from father to son until 1913 when the River Kent froze over and thus technically 'ceased to flow', while an albino deer was born in the deer park. With the terms of the curse thus satisfied a member of the Bagot family, Alan Desmond Bagot, did inherit the Hall from his father.

MUNCASTER CASTLE
(Map reference: 64)

The castle, with its splendid views of the Esk valley, is situated a mile south-east of Ravenglass. Since the 13th century it has been the home of the Pennington family and like a lot of northern houses, it is built round a medieval tower. The pink stone additions were the work of the castle restorer, Anthony Salvin. Today it is famous for its azalea and rhododendron gardens.

The interior can offer 17th-century furniture, sculpture, carpets and a collection of English portrait paintings.

Opening times: Tuesday, Wednesday, Thursday, Sunday and Bank Holiday afternoons from Good Friday to 4 October. The gardens are open on afternoons daily, excluding Fridays, for the same period.
Telephone: Ravenglass 614.

Muncaster Castle is famous for its talisman known as the Luck of Muncaster which must be effective as the same family has been in possession of the castle for seven centuries.

The Luck is a bowl of green-tinted glass, decorated with purple and gold, and is most likely Venetian in origin. It was presented to the Penningtons who owned Muncaster by Henry VI in appreciation of shelter afforded him when he was a fugitive after being deposed in the Wars of the Roses in 1461.

A verse associated with the bowl concludes:

> *In Muncaster Castle good luck shall be*
> *Till this charmed cup is broken.*

The castle has two ghosts. One is that of the luckless King Henry who was murdered in the Tower of London following Edward IV's victory at Tewkesbury. The ghost of the king is said to appear in the chamber where he hid after fleeing north when his rival was first proclaimed king.

The other ghost is headless. He was a young carpenter who forgot his proper station when he fell in love with Helwise, the daughter of Sir Ferdinand Pennington. It would have been better for the youth if the girl had not returned his love but she did, infuriating her father who had already arranged her marriage with a suitable knight.

Sir Ferdinand paid his jester Tom the Fool to assassinate the carpenter. To prove that he had carried out the order, the jester cut off the carpenter's head (perhaps in the castle garden which is now famous for its rhododendrons and azaleas), and showed it to Sir Ferdinand. The master of the castle may have thought that was the end of the matter, but since then the phantom has appeared in his mutilated condition as a mute reminder of the crime.

NAWORTH CASTLE
(Map reference: 65)

Standing to the north-east of Brampton, the castle has many historical associations as befits one of the most effective Border castles. Its walls are medieval, though the interior had to be reconstructed following a fire in 1844.

Visiting by appointment with J. M. Clark and Partners, Bute House, Rosehill, Carlisle.

Old Border ballads refer to 'Naworth's iron towers' and these are still to be seen, the east tower being Lord Howard's Tower and the west Dacre's Tower. In 1577 the castle was inherited by Lady Elizabeth Dacre who, at the age of fourteen, married Lord William Howard who was less than a year her senior. He was to become the famous 'Belted Will' who, according to Sir Walter Scott, earned his nickname by

> *His Bilboa blade, by marchmen felt,*
> *Hung in a broad and studded belt,*
> *Hence, in rude phrase the Borderers still,*
> *Call noble Howard, 'Belted Will'.*

Unlike so many of his kind, Belted Will lived to nearly eighty. Perhaps his toughness can be traced back to the age of nine when he watched while his father, the Duke of Norfolk, was decapitated for plotting on behalf of Mary Queen of Scots.

The event which gave rise to the haunting of Naworth took place some years before Belted Will became Warden. According to the tradition, Lord Dacre of Naworth had an affair with a beautiful but lowborn girl. Unaware of his true name, she gladly gave her heart and body to the gallant lover, believing when she found herself pregnant that he would make an honest woman of her. It was then, in the tradition of deceived maidens, that he told her of his rank and added he could not marry her because a marriage was already arranged with a woman of his station. The girl bore a bastard son, then in despair drowned herself in the stream by the castle on the day her false lover was married.

The next morning Lord Dacre walked out with his new wife and found the girl in the water, her hair streaming about her like Ophelia. At the same time the girl's mother, who had been searching desperately for her daughter through the night, came upon the scene. Blaming Lord Dacre for her daughter's tragedy, she cried a curse which, rather remarkably considering the circumstances, was in rhyme:

> *O curst be the cruel hand*
> *That wrought this hour to me!*
> *May evil grim aye follow him*
> *Until the day he dee.*

Lord Dacre did not live very long after that. Three years after his death, in 1577, his only legitimate son fell from a rocking horse so that, according to a chronicler, 'he had the brains bruised out of his head'.

The male line of the Dacres died out, and the castle passed to Belted Will, through his marriage to Lady Elizabeth, proving the effectiveness of curses to the satisfaction of the locals.

The Naworth ghost is the shade of the girl who drowned herself close to the castle's walls, and it is here that she has been seen in the past. The revenge wreaked by her mother's curse, it seems, did nothing to assuage her restless spirit.

SIZERGH CASTLE
(Map reference: 76)

It is a remarkable thought that a home could be in the possession of one family for seven centuries, yet this is the case with the Stricklands and Sizergh Castle which is to be found three-and-a-half miles south of Kendal. The family has owned the Sizergh site from 1239, though it was not until the middle of the next century that the pele tower was built, around which the present castle grew. In 1450 the Great Hall was added, and further additions were made in the 16th and 18th centuries.

The house offers Elizabethan furnishings and mementoes of Bonnie Prince Charlie. Outside there is an excellent rock garden set out about sixty years ago. Sizergh is now in the care of The National Trust.

Opening times: Wednesday, Sunday and Bank Holiday

Monday afternoons from April to September, and on Thursday afternoons in July and August.
Telephone: Sedgwick 60285.

For long centuries the currents of history have washed round Sizergh Castle, yet its supernatural tradition does not include an armoured knight or a cavalier. This is surprising because a member of the Strickland family, whose ancestor Sir Walter built the original pele tower, carried the banner at the Battle of Agincourt, and during the Wars of the Roses the Stricklands were active Yorkists.

Because of intermarriage with the Parr family during the reign of Edward IV, Katherine Parr lived at the castle before her marriage to Henry VIII. Later the Stricklands supported the Stuarts and with the result that Sir Robert Strickland lost much of his property during the Civil War. His son Charles followed James II into exile yet amazingly the family managed to hold on to Sizergh right up to 1950 when it was presented to The National Trust.

The haunting of the castle seems to be the work of a poltergeist. In one room the floorboards were actually torn up as though by invisible hands, and after they had been replaced they were torn up again. As with so much poltergeist activity there appears to be no rational explanation for the violent manifestations.

Devon

BERRY POMEROY CASTLE
(Map reference: 9)

The ruins of this castle and a once-magnificent mansion are situated in thick woods just north of the A385 between Totnes and Paignton.

Its history goes back to the Norman Conquest when it was built by Ralph Pomeroy who was one of the adventurers who crossed the Channel with William the Conqueror. According to Sir Charles Oman, whose monumental work *Castles* was published in 1926: 'The Pomeroys were among the most powerful of the early Devonian feudal houses and had the unusual luck of continuing their lineal succession for nearly 500 years, though they were more than once in danger of confiscation for treason.'

After the troubles of 1549 the officials of Edward VI confiscated the castle and sold it to the powerful Seymour family. They spent £20,000 (a colossal sum in Tudor times) converting Berry Pomeroy, a task which was never completed. The centre of the castle was demolished to make way for a mansion designed for luxurious living rather than for protection.

During the Civil War the castle was bombarded but, although the walls were 'slighted', the house remained habitable until it was set ablaze by lightning in 1685. Even after this disaster, Sir Edward Seymour was able to entertain William of Orange there after his landing at Brixham on 5 November 1688. Later it was allowed to deteriorate into the romantic ruin which it is today, with its 13th-century gatehouse, turreted walls and façade of the Seymour Lodge with its great windows.

Opening times: Berry Pomeroy is open the year round except at Christmas.
Telephone: Totnes 863397.

The castle's best known haunting began with two sisters, Eleanor and Margaret Pomeroy, falling in love with the same man. Lady Eleanor, the elder of the two, was so jealous of Margaret that she used her power as mistress of the castle to keep her locked in a dungeon beneath one of the towers (now known as Saint Margaret's Tower). The prisoner was allowed so little food that she was a living skeleton before she died in her dark and lonely vault. No doubt the evil Eleanor gloated over the way Margaret's once beautiful features had withered, no doubt she saw her way clear to the heart of the man she desired, but her crime was not to remain a secret – the tormented ghost of her sister from time to time arises from the dead as a reminder of the murder. According to a pamphlet on sale at Berry Pomeroy: 'Now on certain nights of the year, the lovely Margaret is said to arise from her entombed dungeon, leaving Saint Margaret's Tower and walk along the ramparts in long white flowing robes and beckon to the beholder to come and join her in the dungeon below.'

Of the castle's other ghosts, the most sympathetic are a pair of lovers who have been glimpsed vainly trying to touch each other with phantom hands in a room above the gatehouse arch. There are two explanations for their sad tryst. One is simply that a daughter of the household secretly fell in love with a member of a family with whom the Pomeroys had a feud. This Romeo and Juliet situation ended when the girl's younger brother found them together in a rose bower and killed them both for the honour of the Pomeroys.

A more complicated version tells that a certain Lord Berry was strolling with his beautiful cousin Genevieve outside the precincts of the castle when they were set upon by outlaws. Apparently both were knocked unconscious, and Genevieve finally opened her eyes in a dim cave. To her horror she saw bodies lying in grotesque attitudes about her. Then she saw the form of Raby Copeland, Lord Berry's standard-bearer, slumped against the earthen wall.

Using her scarf to staunch the flow of blood from the worst of his wounds, Genevieve listened while the young man whispered how he had followed the robbers to the cave where he had attempted to rescue her. Then he explained that he had found the courage to slay them because of the love he had long felt for her – despite the fact that Lord Berry planned to marry her himself. At this point Genevieve admitted that she had been secretly in love with him and that she would never wed Lord Berry.

When castle retainers carried the standard-bearer back to the castle and placed him in the gatehouse chamber, Genevieve told Lord Berry that she was going to marry Raby. In a frenzy of jealousy the lord of the castle killed his cousin and her wounded lover.

Another Berry Pomeroy ghost is the Blue Lady who, wearing a blue hooded cape, searches the castle grounds for her baby. She was said to have had an incestuous relationship with her father, one of the lords of the castle. When his daughter gave birth to his child he strangled it with his own hands, though another slightly different legend suggests she smothered the infant herself.

One of the best accounts of a haunting at the castle comes down to us from a highly reliable source, Sir Walter Farquhar, whose dedication to medicine was rewarded with a baronetcy in 1796, after which he became physician to the Prince of Wales, later the eccentric Prince Regent. Before the doctor gained his title and his illustrious patient, he lived in Torquay. One day a professional call took him to Berry Pomeroy.

After the wheels of his carriage crunched to a halt by Seymour Lodge – now only a great façade with staring windows – he was shown into a dark but handsomely furnished room. Rays of light filtered through diamond-shaped panes of stained glass, splashing a pattern of luminous colours on a black staircase which led to apartments above.

Minutes passed and just as the doctor began to get impatient a door opened and a young woman entered dressed in a richly embroidered gown. Thinking she was a member of the household come to escort him to the sickroom the doctor took a step forward, but he was completely ignored by the silent girl. Nervously twisting her hands together she crossed to the foot of the stairs, hesitated a moment and then ascended until the light from the window caught her features like a multicoloured spotlight.

Sir Walter afterwards wrote: 'If ever human face exhibited agony and remorse; if ever eye, that index of the soul, portrayed anguish uncheered by hope, and suffering without interval; if ever features betrayed that within the wearer's bosom there dwelt a hell, those features and that being were then presented to me.'

Just after the silent figure appeared to quit the room, the caretaker of the castle walked in, doubtless apologising for the delay, and took the doctor to his wife whose illness was so severe that Sir Walter temporarily forgot the strange figure which had ignored him. When he returned to Berry Pomeroy the next morning he found his patient had rallied, and once out of her bedroom he asked the caretaker about the mysterious young woman he had seen the previous afternoon.

'My poor wife – that it should come to this!' the man exclaimed. And when the doctor tried to ask a question he continued, 'You don't know the strange story – and his lordship is extremely against any allusion ever being made to the tale or any importance being attached to it – but I must and will tell you! You've seen the ghost of the daughter of a former baron of Berry Pomeroy, who bore a child to her own father. In that room above us the fruit of their incestuous intercourse was strangled by the guilty mother. Now, whenever death is about to come to anybody in the castle, the crazed phantom is seen hurrying to the scene of her crime . . . When my son was drowned she was seen – now it is my wife.'

'But your wife is better,' the doctor argued. 'All immediate danger is over.'

The caretaker answered that he had lived in the castle for thirty years, and the omen was always fulfilled.

This talk of the supernatural irritated the medical man – it was, after all, the age of reason – and he said, 'It is absurd to talk about omens. I trust to see your wife recovered.'

But the caretaker's wife died several hours later.

When Sir Walter was one of the most sought after doctors in England, probably on account of his royal connections as much as his medical skill, a lady came to his consulting room to ask his advice about her sister whom she described as 'sinking' through depression following the shock of a supernatural experience. She explained that one morning they had driven from Torquay to Berry Pomeroy to see the romantic ruins with their brother. When they arrived they learned that the caretaker was dangerously ill, in fact he died during their visit.

Not wishing to cause any disturbance at such a time, the lady and her brother went to find the keys for themselves, leaving their sister in a large room in the lodge, with a dark staircase in it.

Having found the keys they returned to find her muttering incoherently about a phantom figure.

'I know that you will say all this is quite preposterous,' the lady said to Sir Walter. 'Indeed, we have tried to treat the matter with scorn and to laugh my sister out of it. But when we joke, she only grows more agitated.'

'I must tell you, before I attend your sister, that this is no delusion,' said Sir Walter. 'I myself have seen the same figure in somewhat similar circumstances. Believe me, it is no joking matter.'

The next day he visited the lady and, with his special understanding of her case, it was not long before she recovered from her malaise. It was not for her the Blue Lady had returned but the caretaker.

A more attractive story concerns an old tree, said to be over a hundred years old, which stands close to the ruined wall of the castle and is known as the Wishing Tree. You have to walk backwards around its trunk three times – being careful not to trip over its gnarled roots – and your wish will be granted.

BUCKLAND ABBEY
(Map reference: 12)

The abbey stands three miles west of Yelverton between the A386 and the River Tavy. In 1541 Sir Richard Grenville purchased the remains of the Benedictine abbey and his grandson turned the church into a mansion thirty years later. In 1581 it was bought by Sir Francis Drake and it is because of this that Buckland is famous. Today his drum is kept here and there are various naval exhibits. The house and its grounds are cared for by The National Trust and the Plymouth Corporation.

> *Opening times:* Weekdays late morning onwards and Sunday afternoons from Good Friday to 30 September.
> *Telephone:* Yelverton 3607.

A curious and frightening manifestation is associated with Buckland Abbey involving a Satanic coach and Sir Francis Drake. Following his circumnavigation of the globe he took up residence at Buckland and it was here, according to legend, that when the Armada threatened England he made a contract with the Devil. Aware of the Spanish naval superiority, Sir Francis may have thought the only possible chance of destroying the seemingly invincible fleet lay in supernatural intervention. It is an interesting point that the tradition suggests he turned to the Father of Lies rather than to God – did he feel that God was already on the side of the Spaniards?

Whatever his reasoning the legend states that for the sake of England he bartered his soul for diabolical aid at the appropriately named Devil's Point where it has been said the phantoms of the sorcerers who assisted in 'arranging' the pact with magical ceremonies still foregather on this headland. As always the Devil kept to his word – the Armada was depleted by winds rather than by English firepower. But the Devil is equally strict about claiming his side of the bargain, and on wild windy nights the phantom of Sir Francis has been seen in an evil black coach, lurching along the route from Tavistock to Plymouth and going through the grounds of the abbey.

The dreaded vehicle is drawn at supernatural speed by a team of traditionally headless horses with a vanguard of equally headless hellhounds, while leaping demons follow behind. I wonder if Sir Francis, surveying England today from the window of his infernal conveyance, wonders whether the sacrifice was worth it?

There is a very old belief that if England is in danger Sir Francis can be summoned to her aid if his drum is beaten, and that if this is done he will re-enter our world at Buckland Abbey. During the Second World War a rumour spread that the old drum had actually been beaten during the air raids on Plymouth.

Dorset

ATHELHAMPTON HALL
(Map reference: 5)

Standing to the east of Puddletown on the A35, the hall's claim to fame is that Thomas Hardy used it as his model for 'Athelhall'. Its history goes back to the late 15th century when it was built for a Lord Mayor of London, Sir William Martyn.

The hall was restored at the end of the last century and some of the present decoration dates back to this. Visitors find that the most impressive feature inside the mellow building is the Great Hall, while outside it is pleasant to wander in the ten acres of formal gardens.

Opening times: On Wednesday, Thursday and Sunday afternoons from Good Friday to 11 October; and on Tuesday and Friday afternoons in August. Also open on Bank Holiday Mondays.
Telephone: Puddletown 363.

Athelhampton Hall has a variety of ghosts – a Grey Lady, a priest in a hooded black robe, phantom duellists and a spectral ape. And for good measure the hammering of a long dead cooper has been heard issuing from an ancient wine cellar whose door is held by locks which came from Newgate Prison.

The most famous ghost is the Grey Lady who has been seen in the Tudor Room. A maid once described her as sitting in a chair there late one afternoon. Thinking that she was a visitor who had stayed on after closing time, the maid told her it was time to go. To the woman's amazement the apparition stood up and vanished through the panelled wall. A housekeeper who saw her on another occasion described her as being clothed in an old-fashioned grey dress and a gauze head-dress. Again she faded away when spoken to.

It is thought that the ghostly monk was really a rector in life who wore a cassock and a 'shovel hat' which gave him his monkish appearance. He was a frequent visitor to the house as he was using it as a setting for a book he was writing, and it seems his interest in Athelhampton has lasted beyond the grave.

More dramatic are the mysterious ghosts who re-enact their duel in the Great Chamber. They are said to play it out until one appears to be wounded in the arm after which they disappear.

In the Great Chamber there is a secret door near the fireplace which opens on to a wooden staircase which leads down to a small storeroom, and up to the Long Gallery. The legend connected with these stairs is that they are haunted by the spectre of a tame monkey which once belonged to one of the Martyn daughters whose ancestors built the house.

As the result of an unhappy love affair she decided that life was too bitter to continue, and she used the secret stairway to go to the room where she could end it all. Her faithful pet followed her when she left the Great Chamber but when she reached the hidden room she shut the door while the animal was still on the steps outside. Remote from the rest of the house the girl took her life, and her corpse was not found for a long time. Meanwhile the poor monkey starved to death in the stairwell.

By a strange coincidence the crest of the Martyn family involved a monkey, depicted holding a mirror in its paw and with the disturbing motto: 'He who looks at Martyn's ape, Martyn's ape shall look at him.'

BETTISCOMBE MANOR
(Map reference: 10)

Situated near Bridport, Bettiscombe Manor mostly dates back to the 17th century, though parts of a building from the previous century are incorporated in it.

Visiting is by appointment only.

A rare but highly dramatic form of English haunting is that involving skulls, some of which have been described as 'screaming skulls' which suggests truly blood-chilling manifestations. Perhaps the most famous skull to have held supernatural power is the one at Burton Agnes Hall, but another which has achieved an eerie fame is the screaming skull of Bettiscombe House.

There are several versions of its story which goes back to the early 18th century though it was not until 1872 that it became widely known. That year a letter from J. S. Udal, a judge and folklore expert, appeared in *Notes and Queries*: 'At a farmhouse in Dorsetshire at the present time is carefully preserved a human skull, which has been there for a period long antecedent to the present tenancy. The peculiar superstition attaching to it is that if it be brought out of the house the house itself would rock to its foundations, whilst the person by whom such an act of desecration was committed would certainly die within the year. It is strangely suggestive of the power of this superstition that through many changes of tenancy and furniture the skull still holds its accustomed place "unmoved and unremoved".'

Following some correspondence in the journal, Mr Udal gave further details: 'The farmhouse (formerly, I believe, an old manor house), now called Bettiscombe House, in which the skull remained, or still remains for ought I know to the contrary, lies in the parish of Bettiscombe, about six miles from Bridport, in Dorsetshire. I cannot ascertain the time when the "ghostly tenant" first took up its abode in the place, but it is tolerably certain that it was some considerable time ago. It has, I understand, been pronounced to be that of a negro; and the legend runs that it belonged to a faithful black servant of an early possessor of the property, a Pinney, who, having resided abroad some years, brought home this memento of a faithful follower.'

This is the most popular account and it goes back to the 17th century when the house was owned by the Reverend John Pinney (an ancestor of the present owner). A Puritan minister, he had been forced to live for some years in Ireland after the Restoration, but finally he was able to return to his home where he lived until 1705.

The politics of the time had cast a tragic shadow over his life. In 1685 his two sons had been involved in the Monmouth Rebellion and were taken before Judge Jeffreys in its bloody aftermath. One was hanged, but the other, by the name of Azariah, was transported as a slave to Leeward Island in the West Indies. After some years he obtained his freedom and prospered, finally returning to Bettiscombe House and bringing with him a black servant. When he was on his deathbed the Negro declared that his spirit would never rest until his body was taken back to the West Indies for burial.

Instead he was buried in the Bettiscombe churchyard, but soon the displeasure of his troubled ghost was felt. In Bettiscombe House there was poltergeist-type activity with doors banging and wild cries echoing through rooms and corridors. Screams were even heard issuing from the servant's tomb. In order to try and stop these disturbances the body was disinterred, and in the process of this its skull became separated.

We do not know if the body was shipped back to the West Indies, but the story goes that the skull was kept in the house, and the terrifying screams were heard again whenever anyone tried to remove it. On one occasion a tenant of the house tried to dispose of the grisly relic by throwing it into a pond, but the disturbances were so bad that he was forced to wade through the water with a rake until he located it in the mud and returned it to its accustomed place.

There is also a legend that the skull was once buried to a depth of nearly ten feet, but somehow it managed to work its way up through the earth until it was found and fearfully replaced. The last time the skull was heard to scream was at the beginning of this century. Then the cries were so loud that, apart from the occupants of the house, they were heard by farmworkers in the fields outside.

There are other explanations for Bettiscombe's restless skull. One is that it belonged to a Negro servant as in the first version, but who then was murdered; another says that the skull only was brought back to England by Azariah Pinney as a *memento mori* of a faithful servant. A completely different story suggests that the skull never belonged to a Negro at all but to a young woman who was murdered at Bettiscombe. Weight was given to the latter version in 1963 when the skull was examined by a professor of anatomy who pronounced it to be the skull of a female in her twenties. Whatever the truth behind the Bettiscombe skull, it seems its power of screaming has kept it where it wishes to be.

CLOUDS HILL
(Map reference: 23)

Tucked away near Wool, one mile north of Bovington Camp, Clouds Hill was the home of Lawrence of Arabia after the First World War when he mysteriously dropped out of public life by becoming an army private. The small house still contains his furniture and other relics, and is a place of pilgrimage for Lawrence enthusiasts. It is in the care of The National Trust.

Opening times: Wednesdays, Thursdays, Fridays and Sundays, afternoons, and Bank Holiday Mondays, from April to the end of September. From October to March the house is open on Sunday afternoons only.

One of the most enigmatic figures of the 20th century is Colonel T. E. Lawrence. Over the years he has been variously regarded as a dashing leader of men with more than a hint of the Desert Song about him, a publicity conscious charlatan and latterly as a man of far greater substance than the hero of Aqaba was ever credited with. His ghost, said to be wearing the Arab dress which made him such a romantic figure when everyone else was in khaki, has been seen in the garden of his beloved cottage.

More frequent is an aural haunting in the vicinity of Clouds Hill – the unmistakable roar of his Brough Superior. This was the motorcycle he was riding when, rounding a bend, he swerved to avoid a couple of boys on bicycles and crashed to his death.

FORDE ABBEY
(Map reference: 35)

The abbey, which is to be found four miles south-east of Chard, was established in 1138 by Cistercian monks and there is still 12th-century work to be seen in the building. Also of architectural interest is the tower and Great Hall which were built by Thomas Chard, the last abbot of Forde, in 1500. After the Dissolution it became the residence of Sir Edmund Prideaux, Cromwell's Attorney General, though little of the exterior was changed in the conversion. Another of the abbey's links with history occurred in 1680 when the Duke of Monmouth used it as his headquarters while preparing his rebellion.

An interesting part of the original abbey is the Norman chapter house which is now used as a chapel.

Opening times: Wednesday and Saturday afternoons from May to September, also Easter Sunday and Bank Holiday

afternoons. In March, April and October the garden is open on Sunday afternoons.
Telephone: South Chard 20231.

The disappointing thing about Forde Abbey is that its resident ghost makes only rare appearances. This is a pity because it seems to be one of those gentle phantoms so in keeping with the peaceful atmosphere surrounding the abbey.

The figure which has been glimpsed in the great hall is thought to be that of Thomas Chard who was abbot of this Cistercian establishment at the time of the Dissolution. He has been described as standing by the large table, his face wearing a pensive expression as he gazes about the place he loved so much during his lifetime.

SANDFORD ORCAS MANOR
(Map reference: 72)

This fine gabled Tudor manor house is to be found in the village of the same name four miles north of Sherborne. Apart from its extraordinary ghosts, its attractions include stained glass, paintings, furniture and fine panelling.

Opening times: Easter Monday, and then Sunday afternoons and Mondays from May to September.
Telephone: Corton Denham 206.

Until it was burnt down in 1939 in fulfilment of a psychic prophecy, Borley Rectory had the reputation of being 'The Most Haunted House in England'; now that distinction must belong to the Tudor manor house at Sandford Orcas. It is said to be haunted by over a dozen ghosts, and has been a happy hunting ground for psychical research groups and television teams alike. And if ever a haunted house looked the part, it is Sandford Orcas with its grey stone walls, deep mullioned windows, tall Elizabethan chimney and high gables, each surmounted by a leering gargoyle in the form of an ape.

When I visited the house I learned of its various spectres from the occupant, Colonel Francis Claridge, whose family motto is encouragingly 'Fear nought but God'. It seems to me that if the manor had only half its complement of ghosts there would still be a lot to fear.

'When my wife and I took a lease on this property we were not informed that it was haunted,' the colonel told me. 'If I'd known what we were going to experience we wouldn't have taken this place. Since then the house has been featured on television and we received many letters from both ex-staff and others confirming many of the various apparitions.'

A Taunton lady wrote that she once slept in the nursery wing when visiting Sandford Orcas and declared that she saw a 'phantom swaying at the foot of her bed'. He appeared to be in evening dress, and she could see him silhouetted against the window.

'His face appeared evil-looking,' she said. 'He stood there for quite a while, then disappeared.'

Mr A. W. Daniell, who lived at the manor with his parents in 1900 when he was aged ten, has described how 'a very nice old lady' visited him on numerous occasions whilst sleeping in the solar which served as his bedroom. Colonel Claridge says that two young ladies related an identical story about the woman who appeared to them when they too had slept in the solar.

There was a considerable amount of publicity about the manor in the mid-sixties, when a BBC television team visited the house and one of its members claimed to have seen the ghost of a man in an old-fashioned farmer's smock and hat.

Later a group from the Paraphysical Laboratory at Downton investigated the house and reported in the *Journal of Paraphysics* that 'a reasonable *prima facie* case had been made out for the hauntings'. They had traced five verifiable cases of haunting experienced by people other than members of the Claridge family.

One evening, after the tourists had finished visiting the manor at about five o'clock, Colonel Claridge was standing outside the house looking over the lawn when he suddenly saw a woman, wearing a dirty macintosh and looking rather like a gipsy in appearance, come through the gate and walk on the grass. He was rather put out that she ignored him and walked on what was a private lawn without bothering to ask permission. Deciding to ask who she was and what she wanted, he stepped forward but as soon as his foot touched the grass the figure melted away.

The lawn featured again when a photograph was taken from it outside the house. It was seen after the negative had been developed that one of the Knoyle sons (the Knoyles owned the manor in the 16th century) had been photographed at the Great Hall window complete with his Stuart hat. He was identified from an old portrait.

On another occasion the ghost of one Edward Knoyle was seen and recognised from a sketch made by a visitor. Other minor apparitions which have been seen at the manor include a lady in a beautiful red silk hand-painted dress from the Georgian period (a similar dress was later found in a chest hidden in the priesthole), a 'little girl in black' who was seen by visitors at the foot of the stairs, and a little dog. Enquiries revealed that he had died in a passage outside the Great Hall in 1900, having been the pet of a woman whose child had been born in the manor. It is said that the fox terrier only appears on the anniversary of his death, but at other times he can be heard running about the nursery.

The idea of a ghostly pet is always rather charming, but this cannot be said for some of the other manifestations which have occurred on this psychically charged spot. For example, there is the phantom rapist . . .

From time to time mysterious tapping sounds have been heard in a room in the staff wing. Soon after the Claridges moved into Sandford Orcas, the colonel's daughter, then aged 25, decided to spend a night in it to see if there was any truth in the story. After she had fallen asleep she was awakened by being hurled to the floor by a supernatural force. She had the sensation of fingers on her throat, and after managing to struggle free from her invisible assailant, was able to race out of the room. She now refuses to enter the house after nightfall.

Infra-red photography has caught the form of this phantom, showing him to be of the Georgian period and seven foot tall.

'This man's pastime in life was raping the maids,' Colonel Claridge told me. 'He will not materialise to any woman who is not a virgin.'

Some of the manor's other frightening apparitions include:

The Screamer: In the back wing of Sandford Orcas Manor is a door with an observation hole cut in it. It was said to be the room where a maniac was held, and during the period from the new moon to the full moon his screams are still sometimes heard in the wing. As a boy he had been sent to Dartmouth College to join the Navy, but while there he killed another cadet. Found to be insane,

46

he was sent back to Sandford Orcas where, during the waxing of the moon, he was restrained.

There is a legend that he died at the age of twenty-seven and was buried secretly in a hidden passage behind the Great Chamber.

'A young man who, with his girl friend, had been round the house on several occasions, asked if he could see a really bad room,' Colonel Claridge told me. 'As we entered this room I stood by the door and felt a most horrible sensation which I could not explain. Then the boy walked in and almost immediately he rushed out in a terrible state of shock and fright, and both I and his girl friend could not get a word out of him for twenty minutes. Then he managed to say that "the man flew at me and tried to kill me". We eventually calmed him down but when he went home after an hour he was still trembling.'

The Suicide: The phantom of this man, who hanged himself from a pulley in the arch of the gatehouse, is said to be visible on a photograph taken on the lawn of the manor. I have seen a blow-up of the picture, which was a typical family snap and which, because of the lack of definition one gets in such pictures when they are enlarged, looks a little blurred. Nevertheless, I found it easy to make out the figure of a man wearing an old-fashioned white milking smock in the background – a figure which, I am assured, was not visible to the person who clicked the shutter. The ghost is said to belong to one of the tenant farmers who took over the house after the Knoyles' long occupation of the manor house came to an end. So-called 'spirit' photographs should be regarded warily for there is nothing easier to fake, yet the spectre of the hanged farmer does not depend on the snapshot only for his authenticity.

Colonel Claridge said that the phantom of this man is often seen walking about the garden.

'On one occasion a lady came with her husband in their car to see the house, and she asked him if she should pay the man sitting in the stables in a white smock,' said Colonel Claridge. 'The husband replied that he could see nothing, and when they came into the house and told us we realised at once that they had seen the farmer.'

It was this ghost which was seen by a member of the BBC television team who felt quite ill with fright when she became aware that it was the suicide's spectre she had seen.

The Moor: A phantom which appeared in the Claridges' bedroom was the figure of a man who materialised briefly for seven nights running. Each time the colonel woke to see him, he appeared to be gazing down on the four-poster before vanishing. When the week was up he did not return for twelve months. Intrigued as to who he was, and armed with a clue as to the anniversary date, Colonel Claridge consulted old records until he came to a murder which had been committed at Sandford Orcas and which tallied with the date of the appearances. The man who appeared looking down on the centuries-old bed was a Moorish servant who had killed his master while he slept by pressing a wire across his throat.

The Wicked Priest: Colonel Claridge has stated that on several occasions he was awakened to see the figure of a priest bending over the great old-fashioned bed in which he and his wife sleep. The phantom seemed to be holding a cloak out as though he was about to smother them. This apparition no longer troubles them since the colonel attached a crucifix to his bedroom door.

I asked him what he thought the significance of this manifestation was: he replied that he believed that at one time the house had been associated with Black Magic, which might account for so much supernatural activity. He believed that the phantom priest had been connected with the performance of the Black Mass. To lend strength to his argument, he showed me some very curious panels of stained glass set in a window which lights one of the main stairways. The scenes included the portrayal of a goat in a way which would have been hard for conventionally-minded Christians to accept a few centuries ago.

The Stinking Man: The most repulsive phantom which haunts Sandford Orcas is that of a man who, during the hour between ten and eleven o'clock at night, moves from the gatehouse and goes through the house to the staff wing where there are four bedrooms. Here he can be heard during the rest of the night, tapping on the bedroom doors five and seven times. He is accompanied by the sounds of bodies being dragged on floors. Colonel Claridge told me that the ghastly thing about this apparition is that when he has passed his quarters he leaves behind him the stench of decaying flesh.

SHERBORNE CASTLE
(Map reference: 75)

The castle is situated a little to the south of Sherborne off the A30. Historically its origins were associated with two unfortunate courtiers, the first being Sir Walter Raleigh. In 1592 Elizabeth I leased the old castle of Sherborne to Raleigh but as he saw the cost of repairing it become increasingly heavy, he decided to spend the money on a completely new residence. This he began in 1594, referring to it as The Lodge.

Raleigh fell from favour and was confined to the Tower of London. Before his execution in 1618 his Sherborne property had been transferred to Sir John Digby. He in turn lost royal favour through his inability to arrange an advantageous royal marriage with Spain. In disgrace he retired to Sherborne where he devoted his time to adding wings to The Lodge, giving it a castle-like appearance. The Digby family has been in continuous occupation of Sherborne since that time.

Today the main apartments are open to the public with good portrait paintings and Georgian furniture on view. Outside, the park has the distinction of being designed by Capability Brown.

Opening times: Thursday, Saturday, Sunday and Bank Holiday afternoons from Easter Saturday to the end of May, and daily afternoons from 1 June to the end of September.
Telephone: Sherborne 3182.

On St Michael's Eve the spectre of Sir Walter Raleigh is reputed to haunt the old garden of Sherborne Castle, where, having done his annual round, the ghost finally dematerialises in the arbour by an oak tree named after him. Perhaps the haunting is in some way connected with the unusual curse which was once laid on the property to prevent it passing into lay hands.

After the Conquest the site was given to Osmund, later the Bishop of Sarum, and a castle was erected on a hill in 1102. A licence to crenellate was granted to the Bishop of Sarum by Richard II in the year of his coronation. This followed a dispute of ownership in which the then bishop challenged the Earl of Salisbury to combat to decide the question.

The matter was finally settled without violence, but in order to ensure the Church's rights to it in the future a curse was invoked on anyone who should wrest it from the bishopric. The imprecation seems to have been effective after Sherborne ceased to be Church property, some of its unlucky owners including the Earl of Somerset and Sir Walter Raleigh who were both executed.

When the castle passed to Baron Digby the curse appears to have spent itself, for his descendants, the Wingfield-Digbys, still own the castle.

WOLFETON HOUSE
(Map reference: 88)

This medieval and Elizabethan manor house is to be found one-and-a-half miles from Dorchester on the A37 leading to Yeovil. It is noted for its splendidly decorated ceilings, fireplaces, wood and stonework and collections of paintings and furniture. For the architecturally-minded there is the Great Hall, interesting stairs and a chapel. There is also a cider house.

> *Opening times:* Tuesday, Wednesday, Sunday and Bank Holiday afternoons from 3 May to 30 September. During August the house is open on afternoons daily, excluding Saturdays. It is possible to visit from October to April by appointment.
> *Telephone:* Dorchester 3500.

Of Wolfeton House's three phantoms the most spectacular is that of Thomas Trenchard who has revisited his earthly home in order to drive a spectral coach and four up the grand staircase – a haunting which seems to be almost identical to that of Hatfield House. Why such a strange act as driving a coach up a staircase should become part of a ghostlore seems strange when it is highly unlikely that this was ever done in reality.

Perhaps its origins go back to a time when grand staircases were a great status symbol and proud manor-owners boasted that their staircases were so huge you could 'drive a coach and horses up them'.

Such a saying might have been remembered in connection with some character who was later reputed to have become a ghost, and in the course of time these two pieces of information became blended into one tradition.

Coach-driving Thomas apart, Wolfeton House has a Grey Lady who has appeared in the gatehouse, and a sad wraith who brings an aura of tragedy to the Great Chamber. She had married into the family who owned the house, and in some long-ago drama committed suicide by cutting her throat.

Hampshire

BEAULIEU ABBEY
(Map reference: 7)

Beaulieu Abbey is in the village of that name, fourteen miles south of Southampton off the B3056. Its famous Motor Museum, with over two hundred exhibits, makes it a Mecca for car enthusiasts and there is always something going on to entertain the visitors, such as daily parades of veteran cars during the summer, a magnificent model railway for children and their fathers, and events such as steam rallies. With these attractions in the grounds it could be that the house itself is overlooked, which would be a pity as it is rewarding to visit.

The rooms open to the public are in Palace House, a 14th-century gatehouse which was restored just over a hundred years ago by the architect Arthur Blomfield.

> *Opening times:* Open daily all year with closing times varying according to season.
> *Telephone:* Beaulieu 612345.

Over half a million people visit Beaulieu Abbey each year but this influx in no way disturbs the extraordinary psychic manifestations which are almost commonplace there. At times the occurrences have been described as very frightening but this is outweighed by the fact that one aspect of Beaulieu's paranormal activity is of breathtaking beauty.

Appropriately there was a supernatural element in the founding of the abbey in 1204. King John, who during his reign was regarded as an enemy of the Church, forced a number of Cistercians to leave their home in Berkshire under pain of having their abbots trampled to death. At the culmination of this persecution the king had a dream in which he and the dispossessed monks stood before a judge who sentenced him to be whipped by the assemblage as punishment for his crimes against them.

He woke in a sweat of terror and found that there were livid welts on his body. He called his chaplain who was quick-witted enough to make the most of this rare moment of royal repentance by suggesting that the way to avoid divine wrath was by reversing his treatment of the Cistercians. The dream must have been a vivid one because the normally fickle monarch never deviated from his act of expiation. He befriended the monks and built them a magnificent abbey at Beaulieu. He became so interested in the project that he frequently visited Hampshire to see its progress of construction, and made it known that he wanted to be buried there.

His wish was not fulfilled but his daughter-in-law Ysabella was interred before the altar in 1230.

The abbey was dedicated with great pomp in the presence of John's son, Henry III, and from then on it enjoyed royal favour until the Dissolution. Edward III granted it an annual tun of wine and it was given the right to offer sanctuary. This meant that any fugitive able to reach the abbey would not be touched by secular law once he or she was within its precincts. Two illustrious persons to make use of this were Margaret of Anjou ('the She Wolf of France') during the Wars of the Roses, and the Countess of Warwick, wife of the Kingmaker, who sought safety there on the eve of the fateful Battle of Barnet and remained for fourteen years.

In 1536 came the Dissolution and Beaulieu Abbey and its lands were sold to one Thomas Wriothesley for £1350, an enormous sum in those days. To the monks whose horizons had been limited to the abbey walls, the sudden end to a centuries-old tradition of work and worship must have been a calamity which is hard for us to imagine. But it is easy to understand that their spirits retained contact with the place which they had so venerated.

The visible haunting of Beaulieu goes back to pre-Dissolution times and comes in the form of a figure in brown (a lay brother as Cistercians wore white habits), by the inexplicable smell of incense and by the sound of chanting.

The ghostly lay brother has been seen on scores of occasions and in 1927 seems to have communicated with a lady walking in the abbey grounds. She must have been psychic because she was convinced that the figure which approached her at dusk told her to excavate in a certain place where she would uncover a box containing bones and stones.

The lady asked Lord Montagu for permission to dig where the spectre had indicated, and when this was carried out the box and its odd contents were discovered just as the ghost had indicated. But such things are hardly regarded as unusual at the abbey.

Until the beginning of the Second World War Beaulieu retained its privilege of having a parish priest who owed no allegiance to a bishop, and the last of these independents styled himself Abbot of Beaulieu and wore ceremonial vestments in keeping with his office. It seems that he was as at home in the ghost world which centres on Beaulieu as in our world of so-called reality. On Christmas Eve he would close the church doors and hold a seance for the ghostly brotherhood. On a typical occasion a member of his flesh-and-blood congregation remarked that a service had been poorly attended whereupon the self-styled abbot retorted it had been packed, obviously referring to his invisible worshippers.

The priest seems to have been very *au fait* with the world of spirits. During the First World War the second Baron Montagu was in the sea for eighteen hours after his ship, the SS *Persia*, had been torpedoed in the Mediterranean. The family only knew that the ship had been lost, and the days which followed were anxious ones. Then the abbot arrived to say that all was well, he had seen the baron walking in front of him, giving the curious explanation that, 'If he were dead he would have been walking behind me.' Soon afterwards news came that Montagu had been rescued.

The brown monk is the most frequently glimpsed apparition at Beaulieu, usually in the cloisters or beyond the medieval winepress. His appearances are not automatic re-enactments because on one occasion he was seen with a scroll. Certainly there is nothing frightening about him, but this is not so of other Beaulieu phenomena.

Miss Montagu, the half-sister of Lord Montagu, once organised some night shooting at Palace House for her film company. There is probably no group more blasé than a film crew, its members give the impression of having been everywhere and seen everything. Whether they are filming a revolution or a new deodorant for a commercial, they only lose their world-weary attitude when discussing a technical problem in their technical jargon. One gets the impression that if they were asked to cover the Last Judgement their main concern would be to find power sockets for their lights.

Such a crew arrived at Beaulieu for Miss Montagu's night location work.

After a few hours a 'sparks' went downstairs to check on a

cable, and returned very hurriedly and palefaced, demanding to know if there was a nightwatchman on the premises. When Miss Montagu shook her head he turned even paler, but seemed unwilling to say what had upset him. For the rest of the night none of the crew would go downstairs alone.

Later, one of Miss Montagu's assistants was going down the stairs when he was aware of footsteps behind him. Thinking it was a colleague he called out something, but to his horror the footfalls caught up with him and then went on ahead although there was no one in sight.

The most spectacular of Beaulieu's hauntings is human voices chanting plainsong. A good description of it was given by the curator of the motor museum who was working late one night in 1959. The air had become thick with tobacco smoke and when he threw open the window to clear it he heard voices in what sounded like a Catholic mass. As it was Christmas week he surmised that the sound was coming from a neighbour's radio. Later he described the chanting as swelling and fading as though the receiver was faulty. As it sounded so beautiful he went across to the dial of his own set in an endeavour to pick up the broadcast but without success.

When he mentioned the sound and how he had failed to pick it up, he was told that it was not an uncommon Beaulieu phenomenon, and that it was usually heard when death had come to someone in the locality. As though to confirm what he had been told he learned that on the night he heard the sound of monks' voices someone had died in the village.

The sounds were also heard on the same night by Beaulieu's catering manageress who, knowing of the death, asked the vicar next day if a special service had been held for the departed. When he said no service had been held the lady realised she had heard the Beaulieu monks.

She said she would always remember the experience because the singing was so lovely, a point which all who have heard it agree upon.

A more melancholy reminder of the old monks is the phantom funeral which is re-enacted at the abbey's ancient burial ground on the north-east side of the church. This, too, is an aural haunting, beginning with the sound of slow footsteps as though several men were carrying a heavy burden, followed by the sounds of a spade.

MOYLES COURT
(Map reference: 63)

Now a school at Ellingham near Ringwood, the exterior of
Moyles Court has hardly changed since it was partly rebuilt after
the Restoration.

Visiting by appointment with the headmaster.

Moyles Court is well known for its aural haunting – the sound of
a lady's footsteps and the rustle of silk. Like the supernatural
echoes of many stately homes, the origin of the phenomenon is
connected with an historical event. In this case the rustling sound
goes back to 1685 when James, Duke of Monmouth, the natural
son of Charles II and Lucy Walter, attempted to usurp the throne
of his uncle James II.

At Taunton *he* had been proclaimed James II, and with an army
of nearly three thousand foot and six hundred horse – mostly
recruited from the peasants and miners of the West Country – he
attempted to surprise a royal army of the same number camped
on Sedgemoor. His brave but inexperienced followers were no
match for the discipline of the king's troops any more than the
Highlanders were a match for the machine-like musket volleys
which swept Culloden.

On the unhappy day of 6 July expert artillery cut bloody lines
through the rebel ranks and seeing the battle was lost almost from
the start, James fled the field. It is said he outdistanced his
companions in his anxiety to quit the scene of the carnage. Two
days later he was caught hiding near Ringwood and taken to his
uncle. Here he grovelled on the floor, offering to become a
Catholic if only his life would be spared.

Kings – or presidents – do not take kindly to those who threaten
their sovereignty. James II was said to have enjoyed the sight of
his nephew's humiliation for an 'indecent time' before he had him
removed to the Tower of London where he kept an appointment
with the headsman on 15 July. The king then unleashed his
revenge on the captured rebels in the form of Judge Jeffreys.

Among those to be brought before the dreaded judge in the
Bloody Assize was Dame Alice Lisle of Moyles Court. The old

lady had not been a supporter of the Monmouth Rebellion, her crime was that for no other motive than pity she had briefly sheltered two fugitives after the rout of Sedgemoor. In court the jury attempted to find her not guilty but they were no match for Jeffreys who bullied them into a verdict of guilty. Dame Alice was sentenced to be burnt at the stake, but James II had the sentence mercifully commuted to straightforward beheading.

The gentle prisoner was housed in the Eclipse Inn at Winchester, and it was from one of its lower windows that she stepped on to the scaffold which had been erected against its wall. To this day her spectre – in this case a slight figure in a brownish dress – haunts the inn, especially the bedroom where she spent her last hours.

Not only does the lady revisit The Eclipse and her old home but there have been stories in the past that she has been glimpsed being driven in a phantom coach in Ellingham Lane close to Moyles Court.

Hereford and Worcester

HARVINGTON HALL
(Map reference: 43)

Of great interest to Roman Catholics, the hall stands four miles south-east of Kidderminster off the A440. This red brick moated Tudor manor house has seven priestholes dating from the time of John Pabinton who built additions to the place in the 1570s. He was a strong Roman Catholic sympathiser, and another legacy from those days of persecution is the upstairs room which once served as a secret chapel. Its walls are still decorated with painted drops of blood, and other rare Elizabethan wallpaintings are to be seen in the passages.

The house has been carefully restored to its present state by the Roman Catholic Archdiocese of Birmingham which owns the hall.

> *Opening times:* Afternoons daily, excluding Mondays, from 1 February to 30 November. The house also opens late mornings from Easter to September.
> *Telephone:* Chaddesley Corbett 267.

When one considers the witch mania which followed the passing of the Elizabethan Witchcraft Act – introduced because conspirators sought to assassinate the queen by magical means – and the number of people who were executed for witchcraft crimes, it is surprising how few ghostly witches there are in Britain. Logically, innocent people who died as a result of the witchfinders' greed would be expected to return out of a sense of outrage. The real witches, and there were certainly plenty of them, would want to return across the frontier of death to wreak revenge on their enemies.

The best haunting of this type I have come across was in the village of Great Leighs in the witch county of Essex where a witch had been buried on a plot of land known as Scrap Faggot Green – Scrap Faggot being the old Essex name for a witch. During the war American army drivers removed the boulder from above her grave in order to drive their heavy tank across the Green – and the ghost of the Scrap Faggot began playing extraordinary tricks on the village. A lot of this malignant activity centred on the St Anne's Castle pub, culminating in a guest fainting when she saw a horrible 'thing' in the fireplace.

The vicinity of Harvington Hall is also the scene for a witch's return. In 1710 one Mistress Hicks was hanged at a nearby crossroads for causing rain to ruin her enemies' harvests and more spectacularly making her neighbours vomit piss. She met her death on the end of a rope because in England the penalty for committing crimes by witchcraft was the gallows rather than the stake and faggots, as in Scotland and on the Continent.

After she was dead Mistress Hicks was buried on the spot, following the old belief that the great cross made by the roads would be a protection from the witch's post mortem activities. At Harvington this theory does not seem to have been effective because since then Mistress Hicks has been seen walking near the hall at dusk.

Hertfordshire

HATFIELD HOUSE
(Map reference: 44)

Hatfield House, at Hatfield, is renowned for its associations with young Elizabeth I. It was her childhood home and she was staying here under threat from her half-sister – whose fanatical anti-Protestant measures had earned her the epithet of Bloody Mary – when the news came that she had inherited the Crown. Soon afterwards she was led on a white horse through the cheering streets of London by handsome Robert Dudley, who had shared her previous tribulations and was now promoted to Master of Horse.

The present house, which is regarded as one of England's finest Jacobean mansions, was the result of an exchange forced upon Robert Cecil, first Earl of Salisbury, by James I. Cecil was persuaded to let the king have his house at Theobalds in return for the Bishop's Palace at Hatfield. He then demolished a lot of the old building and used the bricks for the new edifice which is thought to have been designed by his carpenter Robert Liminge.

Among the historical treasures of Hatfield are two famous portraits of Elizabeth I – and her embroidered hat, silk stockings and gloves – and a posset set which was presented to Queen Mary and her husband Philip of Spain.

> *Opening times:* Afternoons, excepting Mondays and Good Friday, from 25 March to 11 October. (Elizabethan banquets are held in the Old Palace throughout the year.)
> *Telephone:* Hatfield 62823.

One of the fascinating aspects of the British supernatural scene is the number of phantom coaches which have brought terror on midnight roads or appeared as harbingers of doom to inhabitants of ancient houses. Usually they are funereal in appearance with lamps glowing like hellhounds' eyes and are driven by a skeleton or luminous coachman (headless of course) who lashes his black horses (often headless as well) into supernatural speed.

The reason that they have such a place in our folklore is that prior to the spread of the railway system, the coach, whether mail or one belonging to the local gentry, was the fastest and most magnificent vehicle people ever saw. Drivers of crack coaches had a glamour which the airline pilots of today might well envy. The calibre of the horses, the design of the vehicles themselves and record-breaking runs were the subject of many an argument in the village inn, while little boys would imitate the sound of hooves rattling over cobbles rather as they imitate jet engines or racing cars today.

And if coaches with their aura of faraway places and breakneck journeying aroused the admiration of village-bound folk, the idea of a *ghost* coach must have had a great impact upon their imaginations. (Perhaps we have not changed so much as today the public is fascinated by accounts of ghostly aircraft.)

One of the most spectacular coach hauntings has occurred at Hatfield House where a vehicle materialises at the gates and is pulled at furious speed up the drive. At the entrance to the house it passes right through the doors and *continues up the stairway* before fading back to invisibility. What consternation – indeed, heart attacks! – such a surprise appearance must have caused.

In some parts of England it was an old wives' tale that Satan sent a coach to collect the souls of sinners who died unrepentant. Breckles Hall in Norfolk has a tradition based on this odd piece of folklore, concerning the leader of a gang of poachers named George Mace. He had arranged an illicit meeting on the Breckles estate in which his men would gather at an outhouse, to share the game they had taken.

As the moon dipped behind the horizon the poachers duly assembled at the shed, but Mace never arrived. While they were waiting for him they heard the sound of coach wheels on the driveway leading to the Hall's main entrance. What was unnerving about it was the eerie glow which surrounded the vehicle like a halo. From their hiding place the men watched as it pulled up by the front door, then its door was opened, steps were lowered by invisible hands – and then the spectral conveyance vanished.

The poachers slunk home in a gloomy mood, believing that the carriage had come for the spirit of someone who had just died in a state of sin. The following day they learned why their leader had not appeared and why the Devil's coach had visited Breckles Hall.

On the spot where it had halted, the body of George Mace had been found. Jessop, a local author, wrote about it in his book, *Frivola*, concluding: 'There was nothing to show what had killed him. There were no marks of violence on the body nor any signs of sudden illness. His time had come, and he had been fetched away by a Power, which even the boldest poacher cannot hope to defy.'

A double murder committed in the eighteenth century would have passed into oblivion by now if it had not been associated with a spectral coach drawn by a team of black horses. According to the story, the squire of Oulton House in Suffolk returned home after a day's hunting to find his wife in the arms of an army officer The squire attacked the man who had cuckolded him but he was no match for the soldier who killed him and fled, taking the widow with him. The squire's young daughter was left behind. When she grew up she fell in love with a local farmer and a date was set for their wedding.

The night before the ceremony the servants at Oulton Hall saw a strange vehicle draw up out of which stepped a veiled woman carrying a bottle. (Later accounts are more picturesque with the mysterious passenger actually carrying a cup, but I doubt if the springing would have been adequate for her to travel over rough roads without the contents spilling.)

The next morning the bride was found dead, and as the late-night arrival was remembered, it was concluded that the veiled woman was the girl's mother who had returned with poison to prevent her daughter revealing the identity of her father's murderer to her new husband. Since then the coach has reappeared at Oulton, a ghost which has left alive the memory of the tragedy.

Other famous coach hauntings are to be found at the Royal Castle Hotel, Dartmouth; the Kent village of Grafty Green; Ancre Hill in Gwent and at Great Melton and Potter Heigham in Norfolk.

Humberside

BURTON AGNES HALL
(Map reference: 13)

Standing in the village of Burton Agnes, the hall is one of England's least altered Elizabethan country houses. It was designed for Sir Henry Griffith by the celebrated architect Robert Smythson, and was built in the nine years following 1601. One of the great features of Burton Agnes is the carved stone screen in the hall, and the 'Dance of Death' carving over the fireplace in the drawing room. Because the Baynton family has been in possession of the place since 1654 there is a comprehensive collection of period furniture to be seen, but of all the displays probably that of most interest is the collection of early 20th-century paintings.

> *Opening times:* Afternoons excepting Saturdays from 1 April to 31 October.
> *Telephone:* Burton Agnes 324.

As the lid was lifted from the coffin of Anne Griffith, the sexton and gentry gathered about the tomb saw that the shrouded body was in a state of perfect presentation except the head . . . The head, which had somehow become detached from the body, was a gleaming skull. For a minute there was silence, then one of the onlookers conquered his revulsion, bent forward and picked up the skull, taking it back to Burton Agnes Hall where it remains to this day.

The story goes back to the reign of Elizabeth I when Sir Henry Griffith began building Burton Agnes Hall near Driffield in Yorkshire. He lavished such loving care on the project that his three daughters were infected with his enthusiasm and after his death they devoted themselves to extending and improving the property. Of the three the most dedicated was Anne.

The design of the hall was by Inigo Jones and Rubens was responsible for much of the decor. By 1620 the work was completed, but tragically Anne had little time to relax and enjoy her beautiful home. When visiting friends at nearby Harpham, she was – to use a chilling modern word – mugged. She was still alive when she was found and carried to Burton Agnes Hall where for several days she lay dying from her injuries.

During this distressing period Anne's sisters kept watch by her bed, listening to what they considered was her delirious talk. Sometimes she spoke quite rationally, saying that her regret in dying was that it meant quitting the hall which they had all worked so hard to make beautiful. At other times she wildly implored her sisters to keep her head safely in the house so that part of her would remain there for ever.

At first the two women were horrified at the thought, but as Anne raved on and made wild threats about what would happen if her head was taken out of the hall, they gave her their word that they would fulfil her wishes just to calm her. When Anne died her sisters had her buried in the family vault of the Griffiths, not giving a thought to the bizarre promise they had made to hush the unhappy patient's morbid ramblings.

Soon they had reason to remember as a terrible poltergeist force swept through the hall. It reverberated with inexplicable crashes, and in the intervals between them low groans were heard in the corridors, doors opened and then slammed of their own accord until sleep was impossible for the ladies or their terrified servants. They consulted their vicar, explaining their promise to Anne and at the same time expressing their repugnance at the thought of having their sister's corpse exhumed and the ghastly memento placed in their home. The vicar said that if they wanted to have a quiet life at the hall they had better honour their promise.

So it came about that Anne's coffin was opened and her skull was taken to Burton Agnes Hall, whereupon the alarming manifestations ended.

Many years later a maid, new to Burton Agnes Hall and unaware of the story, came across the skull and, with a cry of revulsion, threw it out of a window on to a passing cart. At that moment the horse seemed to be struck by paralysis, and although the farmer belaboured the unfortunate beast, he might just as well have been beating a statue. In the hubbub the girl admitted throwing the relic into the cart. It was found and brought indoors again, whereupon the horse seemed to return to life as though a spell had been lifted from him.

On a later occasion, new and sceptical owners of the hall buried the skull in the garden, but the resulting commotion was so alarming that they hastily retrieved it and returned it to its usual place for safe-keeping.

Such manifestations are not the only haunting connected with Anne Griffith. Occasionally over the years the phantom of a small slender woman in a fawn gown is glimpsed, and is believed to be the ghost of Anne. The last documented account of her appearance was in 1915 and was published in Lord Halifax's *Ghost Book*. He received the account from Mrs Wickham Boynton who was then the owner of Burton Agnes.

'We were having tea in the hall when I looked up and saw a small thin woman dressed in fawn colour come out of the garden, walk very quickly up the steps, and disappear through the front door, which I thought was open, into the house,' wrote Mrs Wickham Boynton. 'I imagined it must be the parson's wife and remarked to my husband, who had seen nothing: "There is Mrs Coutts. Go and bring her in." He went out at once, but presently came back to say that there was no one there and that the front door was shut.'

She then remembered an old story of a fawn lady who had been seen at the hall and who, when she had appeared the last time, had been hurrying up the same steps.

'My father saw her and followed her inside but she had vanished,' Mrs Wickham Boynton continued. 'She is probably the Griffith ancestress, AD 1620, whose skull is still in the house, though no one knows exactly where it is walled up.'

Today if you should visit Burton Agnes Hall you will see a portrait of Anne Griffith with her two sisters hanging above a staircase. Her skull is thought to be placed behind an ancient screen.

EPWORTH OLD RECTORY
(Map reference: 32)

On the outskirts of Epworth village, the Old Rectory is a shrine for Methodists as the home of John and Charles Wesley. It was built of local brick in 1709, and in 1957 – after it had been acquired from the Church of England and restored by the Methodists – it was opened as a memorial to the Wesleys. It is administered by the Trustees of the World Methodist Council.

Opening times: On weekday mornings and afternoons from March to October and on Sunday afternoons only.
Telephone: Epworth 872268.

For two months a mischievous elemental force nicknamed 'Old Jeffrey' plagued the Wesley family at the Epworth rectory. From letters written by the victims emerges one of the best recorded cases of a poltergeist-type haunting, and what adds interest to the accounts is that one member of the family was John Wesley, the founder of Methodism.

At the close of the 17th century John's father, the Reverend Samuel Wesley, took up the living at Epworth in Lincolnshire, a post which is believed to have been the reward for having dedicated a poem to Queen Mary. Here the Reverend Samuel and his large family – he fathered nineteen children – found themselves in a depressing backwater in both senses of the word. Situated in a damp and dreary area of the fens, Epworth was remote and peopled by clannish folk whose leaning towards Presbyterianism made them regard their new High Church vicar with ill-concealed hostility. When he appeared to be relentless on the question of tithes the local peasantry showed their feelings by burning down his barn and then – when he refused to be intimidated by this – his rectory.

The Reverend Samuel was made of stern stuff and instead of quitting Epworth he built a new rectory out of brick, a defiant gesture which won the grudging respect of his parishioners.

The next trouble to beset the Wesleys was of a supernatural nature, but this did not happen until December 1716, when the Reverend Samuel's sons had left home. However, it was still a large establishment with Mrs Wesley, seven daughters and two servants named Robert Brown and Nanny Marshall. It was Nanny who was the first to suffer Old Jeffrey's attentions which 'caused the upstarting of her hair, and made her ears prick forth at an unusual rate'.

Writing to her son Samuel, Mrs Wesley said: 'On the first of December, our maid heard, at the door of the dining-room, several dismal groans like a person in extremis, at the point of death. We gave little heed to her relation and endeavoured to laugh her out of her fears. Some nights (two or three) after, several of the family heard a strange knocking in divers places, usually three or four knocks at a time, and then stayed a little. This continued every night for a fortnight; sometimes it was in the garret, but most commonly in the nursery, or green chamber.'

In an article published later in the *Arminian Magazine*, John Wesley described the early stage of the haunting thus:

'On the second of December, 1716, while Robert Brown, my father's servant, was sitting with one of the maids, a little before ten at night, in the dining-room which opened into the garden, they both heard one knocking at the door. Robert rose and opened it, but could see nobody. Quickly it knocked again and groaned. He opened the door again twice or thrice, the knocking being twice or thrice repeated; but still seeing nothing, and being a little startled, they rose and went up to bed. When Robert came to the top of the garret stairs, he saw a handmill, which was at a little distance, whirled about very swiftly.

'When he was in bed, he heard as it were the gobbling of a turkey cock close to the bedside; and soon after, the sound of one stumbling over his shoes and boots; but there were none there, he had left them below. The next evening, between five and six o'clock, my sister Molly, then about twenty years of age, sitting in the dining-room reading, heard as if it were the door that led into the hall open, and a person walking in, that seemed to have on a silk nightgown, rustling and trailing along. It seemed to walk round her, then to the door, then round again; but she could see nothing.'

This was to be the pattern of the haunting: knockings, horrid gobbling sounds and objects moved as though by invisible hands. And though Nanny had been laughed at on the first day by the Wesley girls, they were soon scared by the phenomenon which they referred to as Old Jeffrey. The only person not affected at the beginning was the Reverend Samuel, and this alarmed his family because it was a tenet of local folklore that in such a haunting the one who was unable to hear the ghostly knocking had but a short while to live.

At first the rector considered it might be some of his parishioners indulging in a new form of protest against his High Church ways – or perhaps it was a trick conceived by his high-spirited daughters to remove the boredom of the bleak fenland winter. Their attitude to the latter explanation was hurt dignity and they said they were 'desirous of its continuance till he was convinced'.

They did not have to wait long. The night after their statement the Reverend Samuel was startled by nine loud knocks which appeared to come from his bedside. This was followed by more raps and bangs, and 'a noise in the room over our heads as if several people were walking'. Mrs Wesley wrote to her son that the disturbance 'was so outrageous that we thought the children would be frightened; so your father and I rose, and went down in the dark to light a candle. Just as we came to the bottom of the broad stairs, having hold of each other, on my side there seemed as if somebody had emptied a bag of money at my feet; and on his, as if all the bottles under the stairs (which were many) had been dashed in a thousand pieces. We passed through the hall into the kitchen, and got a candle and went to see the children, whom we found asleep.'

The rector was now convinced that such manifestations were not the result of human spite or trickery and, fearing it might be the work of a more diabolical agency, he sent his servant to the nearby village of Haxey requesting its vicar to come and help him with an exorcism.

When Mr Hoole, the vicar, arrived at the Epworth rectory he was almost overwhelmed by stories of Old Jeffrey's activities, the most heinous being the noisy interruption of the Reverend Samuel's prayers for the well-being of King George and the Prince of Wales which suggested sinister political undertones. Mr Hoole stayed the night and the knocking which kept him awake so affected his nerves that in the morning he hastened back to Haxey, leaving his host to perform his exorcism alone.

Now Old Jeffrey's manifestations became more menacing. One night Mrs Wesley saw something scuttle from beneath her bed . . . something which she described as 'like a badger, only without any head that was discernible'. The same apparition appeared to the servant Robert Brown, and on another occasion something resembling a white rabbit 'turned round before him several times'.

Once when he was grinding corn in a garret Robert paused in his work and saw that the mill's handle continued to spin as though worked by an unseen force. Later Robert declared boldly that 'nothing vexed him but the mill was empty. If corn had been in it, Old Jeffrey might have ground the heart out of him . . .' Brave words – when everything seemed back to normal!

Meanwhile a new aspect of the haunting was the brushing of something against members of the household in the dark. The Reverend Samuel declared: 'Thrice I have been pushed by an invisible power, once against the corner of my desk in the study, a second time against the door of the matted chamber, a third time against the right side of the frame of my study door.'

Despite everything the clerical mind of the rector could devise – prayers, exorcism and speeches to the 'ghost' asking it to leave – Old Jeffrey continued to play his tricks over Christmas and into the New Year. Then, two months after Nanny had been frightened by the first knockings, the phenomenon ceased as inexplicably and as abruptly as it had begun.

Kent

EYHORNE MANOR
(Map reference: 33)

The manor is placed five miles east of Maidstone, just north of the A20 on the B2613. It is a timber-framed house from the early 15th century, and a model is kept to demonstrate the framework. The most unusual attraction is a museum of laundry equipment, while outside there is a herb garden planted in the style of the 17th century.

> *Opening times:* Saturday and Sunday afternoons from Good Friday to 30 September, and Tuesday, Wednesday and Thursday afternoons in August.

Eyhorne Manor – once the home of Catharine Howard – has a fascinating range of supernatural manifestations. The most interesting, and creepy, of these is a 'slithering sound' as though a large piece of invisible silk is being dragged across the floor. Mrs Sheila Simmonds who with her husband owns the manor, has described the slithering as being 'not very nice' when on several occasions it has seemed to be coming towards her. Such a description must be an understatement, and no wonder she found it necessary to run into the garden to escape it.

A lady who lived in one of the cottages which then made up the manor in the 1940s was alarmed by the sound of footsteps on the stairs where there was no visible person who could have been the cause of them. She was even more disturbed when her four-year-old daughter asked her one evening if the 'little old lady' would be coming to see her that night. The child added that the old lady told her stories but because she whispered she was unable to hear them properly. On several occasions the mother crept to the door and heard her daughter speaking to the 'grey lady'.

Understandably it was decided to move the child to another room but for some time she was upset because she missed the nocturnal visits of the ghost. A neighbour once saw the grey lady gliding along a passage.

The same tenant was working in the garden one day when she noticed a small man in black regarding her closely. Thinking he was a visitor she greeted him and for a moment looked down at her weeding. When she looked up again he had vanished. From then on she found that a dog which frequented the garden would bark at the spot where the figure had briefly materialised.

A more amazing phenomenon seems to have been inspired by a poltergeist rather than a phantom. One day the tenant saw a peg detach itself from the clothesline, fall to the ground – and disappear. Despite a thorough search of the ground beneath the line the peg was never seen again.

Similar manifestations occurred when the present owners were carrying out a programme of restoration on the manor. Objects – ranging from a spoon to a raincoat – would rise in the air as though lifted by invisible fingers and then drop as if suddenly released. Sometimes small objects – such as a pair of scissors – would vanish during a moment when the person using them had turned away, only to reappear days later in some unlikely spot. In the case of the scissors they were found lying on the lawn without the slightest hint of rust.

Such disappearances and reappearances are not unique to Eyhorne. I remember the landlady of The Black Horse in nearby Pluckly (known as England's most haunted village) describing exactly the same apporting of the pub's keys. One wonders into which dimension such objects could be hidden and what sort of entity appears to enjoy simple practical jokes.

HALL PLACE
(Map reference: 40)

Built in 1540, this historic mansion stands in the London Borough of Bexley at the junction of the A2 and the A223. Of interest to the visitor inside is the Great Hall, a three-hundred-year-old staircase and a plaster ceiling equally old. Outside various gardens, including water, rock and peat ones, are open during daylight hours.

Opening times: Weekdays all the year round and Sunday afternoons from April to September.

It is the sound of heart-rending cries which is the supernatural manifestation connected with the tower at Hall Place. The haunting goes back to when Lady Constance watched while her husband Sir Thomas Hall was gored to death by a stag which had been brought into the courtyard. In her anguish she ran up the steps to the top of the tower where she launched herself into space.

Not only does the grief of the poor suicide linger in the tower, a misty figure has been seen in its vicinity. This could be the spectre of a previous owner Sir John Dashwood whose lifestyle was in keeping with that of his brother, Sir Francis Dashwood, who organised the Hell Fire Club in the caves of High Wycombe.

A much more famous ghost associated with the house is Edward, the son of Edward III, and known in history as the Black Prince. He stayed at Hall Place before leaving to campaign in France, and one wonders what was the strange attraction which drew him back there after death. For centuries he has been regarded as a harbinger of doom, his appearances warning the owners of the house when some calamity is about to befall them, or that England is endangered. Dressed in his black armour, he has usually been seen at midnight. Such appearances have been accompanied by what sounds like faint medieval music.

Lady Limerick, who resided at the hall some years ago, was convinced that she had glimpsed this ghost on four occasions prior to tribulation coming to her family. During the Second World War there were stories of the phantom prince being seen just before British reverses.

HEVER CASTLE
(Map reference: 47)

Two miles east of Edenbridge there is a small but exquisite castle which is most famous for its associations with Anne Boleyn. Hever was begun towards the end of the 14th century by Sir John de Cobham and improved during the next two centuries by the Bullen – or Boleyn – family. Until Anne's marriage to the king, royalty had frequently been guests at the castle, but following her execution it seemed as though a blight had fallen upon it. In the late Victorian era its circumstances had decayed to such a point that it was used as a farmhouse.

In 1903 William Waldorf Astor bought the place, restoring its outward appearance and rebuilding the interior in the style of the 16th century. An Italian garden was laid out which today makes a splendid setting for a collection of Roman statuary.

Opening times: Tuesday, Wednesday, Friday and Sunday afternoons, from 29 March to 27 September. The castle is also open on Bank Holiday Mondays but not on Good Friday.
Telephone: Edenbridge 862205.

Hever Castle has everything for the tourist and the visitor: the interior of a stately home complete with period furniture, works of art and historical treasures, and a collection of medieval instruments of torture, discipline and execution. In the vast grounds outside there is a maze, a superb Italian garden, a reconstructed Tudor village, the Park Wood (with a smuggler's cave) and a loggia with a colonnaded piazza which looks over a thirty-five-acre lake which took two years to excavate. But, above all, the castle has the ghost of Anne Boleyn.

Nearly four and a half centuries have passed since her execution in the Tower of London, yet her fascination as a woman and an historical character remains. The love Henry VIII felt for her led to the English Reformation, she became the mother of Elizabeth I, and her death at the age of thirty-two placed her among the tragic but fascinating quartet of British queens who have knelt at the headsman's block.

Anne – just returned from the French court – met King Henry in the castle garden. His passion for her began in 1522, though he continued to treat his wife Queen Catherine of Aragon with suitable respect until 1527. From the example of Elizabeth Woodville's association with Edward IV, Anne knew that virtue could sometimes be more profitable than vice, and she determined not to emulate her sister who had been a mistress of the king. If Henry wanted her he would have to marry her.

Henry enjoyed wooing an elusive lady – it was different from anything he had experienced before. He wrote lengthy letters to her and composed a poem in which he compared her to a holly, part of which ran:

Now unto my lady
  Promise to her I make
For all other only
  To her I me betake.

His sentiments showed more vividly when he wrote: 'Mine own sweetheart, this shall be to advertise you of the great elengeness (loneliness) that I find here since your departing. I think your kindness and my fervencies of love causeth it; for otherwise I would not have thought it possible that for so little a while it should have grieved me. Wishing myself (especially of an evening) in my sweetheart's arms, whose pretty dukkys I facest shortly to kiss.'

When one contrasts this letter with the fate of Anne, one cannot help being reminded of the Earl of Stafford's remark: 'Put not your trust in princes . . .'

While Henry strove to divorce his queen, Anne was created Marchioness of Pembroke, travelled with the royal retinue and had her own apartments. When she knew she had sufficient hold on the king she allowed him her favours, and she was pregnant when Henry secretly married her in January 1533.

With the Reformation under way, the Convocation obediently acknowledged the invalidity of Henry's marriage to his first wife the following April, and the next month Archbishop Cranmer confirmed the king's marriage with Anne. In June he placed the crown on her head.

Yet within three months of this Henry's love for her began to cool, and the birth in September of a daughter named Elizabeth did not revive it. The next year Anne's hopes of producing an heir were dashed when she had a miscarriage, and the king solaced himself by falling in love with one of her maids of honour, Jane Seymour. After this her progress to the Tower was inevitable.

Following the execution, Anne's ghost has frequently returned to Hever to glide over a bridge which spans the River Eden in the castle grounds. On each occasion the appearance of the spectre has been reported on Christmas Eve.

Anne's father, Sir Thomas, continued to live in disgrace at Hever until his death in 1538 when the king annexed it and two years later granted it to Anne of Cleves whom he had just divorced. After this the glory of Hever faded until 1903 when it was bought by William Waldorf Astor – later created the first

Viscount Astor of Hever Castle – who began a programme of restoration. The size of the undertaking can be gauged by the fact that it took 2000 workmen four years to give it the appearance it has today.

IGHTHAM MOTE
(Map reference: 51)

In the village of Ivy Hatch, off the A227 south-east of Sevenoaks, this house is a remarkable example of an ancient moated manor house. The Great Hall was built in the 14th century and also of architectural interest is the Tudor chapel which was built around 1520.

> *Opening times:* Friday afternoons the year round, and Sunday afternoons from April to September.
> *Telephone:* Sevenoaks 62235.

A little over a century ago renovations were being carried out at Ightham Mote when the carpenters found a sealed cupboard which had been made to look as though it was part of a wall. When they attacked it with chisels and crowbars the door swung open and to their horror they saw that it contained a skeleton – a skeleton whose position suggested that it was the remains of someone who had been imprisoned alive.

Medical examination indicated that it was a female skeleton and immediately speculation began as to whether these bones had belonged to the famous ghost of Ightham. This phantom was called Dorothy Selby in life and is believed to be the anonymous author of the letter sent to her cousin Lord Monteagle warning him of the Gunpowder Plot of 1605.

Legend says that friends of the conspirators walled up the unfortunate Dorothy as an act of revenge.

LEEDS CASTLE
(Map reference: 54)

Surrounded by a beautiful estate off the A20, four miles east of Maidstone, the castle is said to be named after Led, the chief minister of King Ethelbert IV of Kent in AD 857. It was built on two islands in the centre of a lake and is known as 'the castle of the medieval Queens of England' because of its early associations with royalty. These were taken further when Henry VIII made it into a royal palace.

Much rebuilding was carried out in the early part of the 18th century when the castle's outer walls were removed to ground level in order to enhance the view of the lake moat. In 1974 the Hon. Lady Baillie willed the estate to the Leeds Castle Foundation which is a charitable trust aiming to preserve the beauty of the castle and its grounds for the public, and to promote outstanding achievement in medical science.

Opening times: Tuesday, Wednesday, Thursday and Sunday afternoons, and Bank Holiday Mondays, from April to October.
Telephone: Maidstone 65400.

It was the appearance of an evil black hound which struck fear into the hearts of the occupants of Leeds Castle, for they knew that a sighting of the ghostly animal was inevitably followed by ill-fortune. It could be that this Baskerville-like harbinger was in some way connected with Eleanor of Gloucester, the aunt of Henry VI. In 1431 this lady was found guilty of having practised 'necromancy, witchcraft, heresy and treason', and was sentenced to spend the rest of her life imprisoned in the castle.

LYMPNE CASTLE
(Map reference: 59)

Off the B2067 three miles north-west of Hythe, the site of this interesting medieval castle goes right back into Roman, Saxon and Norman history. Around 1360 the castle was rebuilt from an earlier fortification, overlooking the ancient Roman Shore Fort known as Stutfall Castle. It commands an advantageous view across the Romney Marshes and across the Channel to France. The building was restored in 1905.

Opening times: Daily from June to September, and on Bank Holiday weekends.

Lympne Castle boasts one of Britain's oldest ghosts, a Roman soldier who is heard climbing the East Tower to do sentry duty. It is surmised that he accidentally fell to his death because although his footfalls ring on the steps as he goes up – as Peter Underwood points out in his *Gazetteer of British Ghosts* – they are never heard coming down.

As the present castle was built on the ruins of a Roman watch tower it is easy to understand why this haunting has continued down the ages. Ancient history was also the background to the six ghostly shapes which have been glimpsed within the castle walls. They are linked to the tradition that six fugitive Saxons were slain here by Norman soldiers after the Conquest.

Prior to 1947, Henry Beecham, the brother of Sir Thomas Beecham, and his wife resided in the castle, and it was Mrs Beecham who saw another of the castle's ghosts. She described it as a priest 'with grave sad eyes' standing in a small room in the West Tower.

SCOTNEY CASTLE
(Map reference: 73)

Under two miles south-east of Lamberhurst on the A21, this fairy tale castle is hidden away in a deep wooded valley. The reflection of its ancient Ashburnham Tower shares the moat along with waterlilies, and the scene is so picturesque it could be a film set. The castle goes back to 1378 when Roger Ashburnham commenced building it, but only the tower which was named after him remains today. He had planned Scotney as a residence rather than a castle, but after the French burned Hastings and sacked Rye he decided to fortify it.

In 1411 the castle passed into the ownership of the Darrell family who held it for three-and-a-half centuries. As they were ardent Catholics, Scotney became the secret headquarters for the Jesuit 'missionary' Father Blount in 1591. During his seven-year stay he was twice nearly captured and his narrow escapes are detailed in the castle guide book. In 1836 Edward Hussey, the then owner of the estate, decided to build a new house on the site and employed the celebrated architect Anthony Salvin.

Today Scotney is in the care of The National Trust.

Opening times: The gardens only are open to the public on Wednesday to Sunday afternoons, and on Bank Holiday Mondays, from April to October.
Telephone: Lamberhurst 890306.

On a fine English summer's day I can think of no more beautiful sight than that of Scotney Castle dreaming above its reflection in a lily-starred moat. It has just the right romantic style of architecture, blended with a sense of gentle decay that only time can bestow.

The riddle connected with this delightful place occurred on 12 December 1720, at the funeral of Arthur Darrell who had died while on the Continent. When the coffin was lowered into the grave the mourners noticed in their midst a stranger muffled in a black cloak and as the clods began to thud on the coffin lid, this unknown spectator remarked, 'That is me they think they are burying!' After these extraordinary words he vanished. According to some accounts, he disappeared before their eyes.

Was it the ghost of Arthur Darrell, or was he still alive with some secret reason for wishing to be thought dead?

John Bailey, a sexton who died in 1867, claimed that when he was preparing a grave in the Scotney Chapel of Lamberhurst Church he came upon an iron-studded coffin unexpectedly and, prising off the lid to try and find out who it contained, saw it to be full of stones. We cannot be certain that this was Arthur's coffin, and if it was why did he risk detection by attending his own funeral? The riddle of Scotney remains unsolved.

Scotney's resident ghost appears as a figure crawling painfully from the moat. The eerie phenomenon is glimpsed only on dark nights, the reason being that he was an excise officer who was killed by a band of smugglers on a moonless night when he surprised them with a pack train of contraband.

His body was thrown in the moat. Now its ghostly shape materialises in the water and, festooned with waterweed, climbs up the bank and makes its way to the door of the castle before dissolving and leaving a dank miasma behind it.

Lancashire

CHINGLE HALL
(Map reference: 21)

Situated at Goosnargh, near Preston, Chingle Hall is a small manor house which, according to the *Historic House Handbook*, 'is said to be the most haunted house in Britain'. It is believed to go back to 1260 when it was built by Adam de Singleton. Certainly its oaken front door is seven hundred years old. One of its interesting features is that its secret rooms are open for the public to see.

> *Opening times:* Apart from Mondays and Fridays, it is open on afternoons all the year round.
> *Telephone:* Goosnargh 216.

Chingle Hall's main claim to fame is that it was a secret centre for Catholicism after the Reformation. It is to be expected, therefore, that its phantoms have a clerical flavour and indeed the ghost frequently seen in the haunted room upstairs is that of a Franciscan monk. Although no one can say with certainty who he was in life, many believe that he is the spectre of St John Wall.

In 1679 this Catholic hero was put to death at Worcester, and after the execution his head was taken secretly to France where it was venerated as a holy relic. When the Revolution broke out a number of nuns escaped from the terror to England, bringing with them the head of the saint. The question is, did they take it back to France for interment when they returned across the Channel in 1834, or was it taken and hidden in some secret niche in Chingle Hall where John Wall had been born?

Strength is given to the latter proposition by the fact that, despite intensive searches in France, the missing head has never been located.

Apart from the ghost – which may be that of a saint – the hall is the scene of other supernatural occurrences. Invisible footsteps have been heard echoing from the stone bridge which stands in place of the drawbridge, through the house, up the staircase and into a small room where they fade away. On one occasion these phantom footfalls were heard simultaneously by nine people, an unusual happening as a multiple experience of ghostly phenomena is comparatively rare.

Another strange manifestation occurred in 1968 when two boys in the famous haunted room were scared by knocking sounds and the appearance of a light 'the size of a hand' which glowed in the middle of the room before vanishing into the wall. In his book, *Our Haunted Kingdom*, Andrew Green asks whether this could be a sign as to the hiding place of John Wall's head.

HALL-I'-TH'-WOOD
(Map reference: 39)

Standing off Crompton Way on the north side of Bolton this 15th-century manor house is quite extraordinary for the patterns which cover its walls between the timber framing. Additions were made in the 16th and 17th centuries though nothing has been added to it since 1639. It owes its present condition to Lord Leverhulme who restored it with dedicated care, furnishing it as a yeoman's house would have been three centuries ago.

Opening times: Daily excluding Thursdays and Sundays, the year round, and also Sunday afternoons from April to the end of September.
Telephone: Bolton 51159.

Hall-i'-th'-Wood must have been a perfect setting for the recounting of Christmas ghost stories because its own supernatural manifestations begin at Christmas, continue during the festive season but stop at Twelfth Night. The seasonal ghost is a cavalier who runs up the great staircase. This much is known because in the past he has been seen, though for a long time now his presence has been marked only by the sound of his hurried footsteps.

In the past he has been described as 'racing' up the stairs though no one knows why he should be in such haste. One theory is that in life he came to the hall to retrieve some piece of evidence which could be used against him or his family after the Royalist cause was lost.

The reason he would not want it to remain at Hall-i'-th'-Wood was because the house came into the possession of one Christopher Norris who had the lucrative job of administering the ex-Royalist estates which had been 'nationalised' in Lancashire. Certainly ghosts from former days must have been furious that their homes should pass into such hands and perhaps in some way the Christmas haunting has some connection with that. Who can say? The centuries have passed, old resentments have been forgotten in the living world and the activities of the ghostly cavalier are now merely puzzling.

As with so many hauntings, it seems strange that some ordinary action – such as running upstairs or merely walking on a path – should be imprinted on the tape of time while thousands of more significant actions made by a ghost in his or her lifetime are consigned to oblivion once that person's memory fades. It does suggest that what is significant to us has little meaning in the psychic world.

RUFFORD OLD HALL
(Map reference: 69)

Described as one of the finest existing buildings from the 15th century, the hall is at Rufford six miles north-east of Ormskirk. The oldest part is the timber-framed Great Hall, whose walls are ornately decorated, and which is notable for its hammer-beam roof and unique screen believed to be the only movable one still intact.

For the visitor there are collections of arms and armour, 17th-century oak furniture, tapestries and coins. There is also a museum depicting aspects of rural life in Lancashire from prehistoric to Victorian times. The house is now in the care of The National Trust.

Opening times: Afternoons daily excluding Mondays from March to December, but closed on Wednesdays during March and from 1 October onwards.
Telephone: Rufford 821254.

It was the lighting of the Ashurst Beacon which started a chain of events which was responsible for the appearances of the Lady in Grey at Rufford Old Hall. In the past the beacon was a signal for mobilisation against the Scots, and its gleam put a sudden end to a jolly engagement party being held at the hall. It meant an immediate departure for the new fiancé of Elizabeth Hesketh whose family remained the owners of Rufford until 1936.

The young soldier rode off to the war and for several gloomy weeks Elizabeth waited to get word of him. Finally a messenger arrived with the news that the campaign had come to a successful conclusion and that soon her fiancé would be returning to Lancashire. The Heskeths began to prepare for the wedding which was planned to take place immediately on his arrival, but instead of the bridegroom galloping in from the North, another messenger arrived with the news that he had been slain in the fighting after all.

The girl refused to believe it. Surely the second messenger was just as likely to be wrong as the first! She declared that the wedding would still take place and her family, alarmed by her mental condition, humoured her by continuing the preparations. The days passed and Elizabeth watched for her lover's return with feverish eyes, and even when she fell fatally ill she still refused to believe that he was among the slain.

Elizabeth still haunts Rufford Old Hall, one of her most dramatic sightings being in the music room. She is still waiting . . .

SAMLESBURY HALL
(Map reference: 71)

On the A677 four miles east of Preston is this 15th-century timber-framed building with black and white exterior decoration. Much restoration work was carried out in 1835 with considerable rebuilding in brick. The hall is used as an exhibition centre and the Council for the Preservation of Rural England have an antique shop there. In the Great Hall is part of a screen similar to the one at Rufford Old Hall and which goes back to 1532. The grounds have a nature trail, a pleasant old water garden and a field for archery.

Opening times: Daily, excluding Monday, all the year round. The house is also open on Bank Holiday Mondays.
Telephone: Mellor 2010.

There is a Romeo and Juliet element in the sad story of the White Lady of Samlesbury Hall. Her apparition is frequently reported not only in the fine old manor house but in its grounds and sometimes on the road which runs past it. On several occasions drivers claim to have seen her semi-transparent shape fixed briefly in the beams of their headlights.

Her name was Dorothy Southwood and she lived at Samlesbury in Tudor times when the question of religion had split the country apart. The Southwoods were staunch Roman Catholics and not afraid to take terrible risks for their faith. They frequently sheltered fugitive Jesuits, and among their sons was St John Southwood who in 1654 was put to death at Igham.

With such a family background it was hard for Dorothy when she fell in love with a young member of the Hoghton family who lived in nearby Hoghton Tower. They were as fanatically Protestant as the Southwoods were Catholic. As was to be expected both families put every obstacle in the way of the young lovers who were forced to meet by stealth in the grounds of the hall.

Before long the family pressure on both sides became intolerable and at a midnight meeting in the garden Dorothy and her lover planned to elope, not knowing that her brother was hidden in the shadows listening to their whispers.

The result was that when young Hoghton arrived to bear away his bride the brother was waiting for him with a sword. Dorothy's smile of welcome froze as she saw her brother emerge from the bushes and run his sword through the youth. The victim was buried close to a wall of the house and Dorothy was packed off to a convent where she wasted away until she died of sorrow.

Since then her wraith revisits Samlesbury Hall, particularly the spot young Hoghton was buried where she continues to weep audibly for him.

A typical experience of this was recounted by a colonel who was staying at Samlesbury towards the end of the last century. He woke during the night to hear the sound of crying in the next room and assumed that a sick person must be in pain. In the morning he mentioned it to his host who explained that the room was in fact empty and what he had heard could only have been the lamentations of the White Lady.

At the beginning of the last century some men were digging drains when they unearthed a skeleton close to the wall where tradition stated that Dorothy's lover had been secretly interred.

There is also a story connected with the hall that once a priest was discovered hiding there and killed on the spot, bloodstains on the wooden floor remaining until Victorian times when the owner had the boards replaced to calm his superstitious servants.

SMITHILLS HALL
(Map reference: 77)

In a large park on Smithills Dean Road in Bolton stands the old medieval house – with its Victorian additions – called Smithills Hall. Its Great Hall goes back to the first half of the 15th century and its east wing which was constructed about a hundred years later houses a collection of good oak furniture.

> *Opening times:* Weekdays and Sunday afternoons all the year round except Christmas and Boxing Day, New Year's Day and 13 April.
> *Telephone:* Bolton 41265.

The clerical ghost which has been seen to pass through the green room at Smithills Hall goes back to the 16th century when many people were prepared to die – and frequently did – for religious conviction. The spectre of Smithills is believed to be George Marsh, a farmer who forsook the land to become a priest. His rugged individuality and outspoken doctrines were at variance with what was officially acceptable in those days. Queen Mary, that sad, cruel religious fanatic, took exception to his preaching and the Earl of Derby was dispatched to arrest him on a heresy charge.

Knowing only too well the hideous outcome which usually followed such accusations, Marsh prepared to flee across the Channel when word reached him that the earl was on his way. Then he learned that his mother was being held as his accomplice and his filial duty overcame his personal fear. He gave himself up to the authorities and was taken to Smithills Hall whose owner was a magistrate named Robert Barton.

The hearing took place in an upper room of the house where the priest was finally found guilty of heresy – that is, not agreeing with the majority – and as this was a crime worse than murder he was sentenced to be burnt to death.

While being escorted through the chapel passage to the place of execution the injustice of the situation overcame him and, rather like Galileo, he stamped his foot as an expression of his feelings. As a result his footprint, which tradition asserts was 'bloody', remained fixed on the stone floor.

London

CHARLTON HOUSE
(Map reference: 19)

A Day Centre at Greenwich, Charlton House is regarded as one of the most important Jacobean houses left in London.

Visiting is by appointment with the Warden.
Telephone: 01-856 3951.

The ghost of Charlton House may have given up his earthly life two and a half centuries ago, but one aspect of the flesh has remained, and that is his passion for the opposite sex. The amorous phantom is that of Sir William Longhorne, Governor of Madras, who bought the house as an 'asylum for his old age'. Despite all his attempts he never managed to father an heir to inherit Charlton, and it seems his obsession with the process has lasted beyond the tomb.

It is said that he haunts the passages of the house in search for young women and causes the doorknobs of their bedrooms to turn as though he is trying to enter.

During the First World War Charlton was converted into a military hospital and the owner, Lady Wilson, told the nursing staff not to put patients in a certain bedroom which had the reputation of being the haunt of the Charlton ghost. As the flow of casualties increased from the Western Front her advice had to be disregarded, with the result that many of the wounded declared that they had glimpsed the phantom there.

Part of the house was damaged by bombs during the Second World War, and later, when rebuilding work was being carried out, a pathetic discovery was made. It was the mummified body of an infant which had been concealed in one of the ancient brick chimneys.

Some time later a local lady was walking in the grounds of Charlton House when she saw what appeared to be a servant girl in old fashioned costume with a dead baby cradled in her arms. What hints of forgotten sorrow the appearance of ghosts sometimes revive!

An odd story connected with the house was recalled by the author W. T. Vincent who wrote, 'Lord Downe, who dwelt at Charlton House in the reign of Charles II, was seated at the great fireplace, which is always kept polished like a mirror, when he saw the reflection of some villains engaged in a robbery on the Heath. He called his servants, and despatched them with such promptitude that they arrested the ruffians and brought them to justice.'

KENSINGTON PALACE
(Map reference: 52)

In Palace Avenue, off Kensington High Street, the palace is a group of brick buildings which have been a royal residence since 1696 when Christopher Wren supervised its reconstruction for William and Mary. George I had further additions made, and later on it was the birthplace and childhood home of Queen Victoria – her dolls and toys are still to be seen. Although it is still used by members of royalty, the State Apartments have been open to the public since 1899.

Opening times: Department of the Environment standard hours.

George II, who was Elector of Hanover as well as King of Great Britain and Ireland, was the last monarch to return as a ghost. Like his father, George greatly preferred his German territory, and as he lay dying at Kensington Palace in October 1760 his main preoccupation seemed to be the delay in the arrival of dispatches from Hanover. This was because the wind was in the wrong direction, making it impossible for the ship bringing a courier to cross the Channel.

Through the window of his apartment the king watched the weather-vane (in the shape of a bird atop the clock tower) hoping for a change in the wind, and demanding of his servants in his heavy accent: 'Vy don't dey come?'

When the wind changed and the dispatches came, it was too late. The king had died on 25 October. His phantom has since been reported at Kensington Palace gazing at the vane to see if the wind was changing.

THE TOWER OF LONDON
(Map reference: 81)

For the last nine centuries the Tower has been an enigmatic symbol of London – it has protected its citizens and it has been feared by them. In the past its great keep and towers have thrown a shadow of terror across the land – today it is a place of entertainment. It is the world's best known castle, and the best loved by tourists. Here one can see the block and axe which were once such a significant feature of English politics, and – for an extra charge – the crown which was worn by Her Majesty the Queen at her coronation along with the other Crown Jewels.

William the Conqueror built the White Tower and the two encircling walls and defensive towers were added by later monarchs – the first, or inner, wall being the work of Richard I and Henry II while the outer one was built by Edward I. Although these ramparts have been frequently rebuilt over the centuries their original layout has not changed.

Today the White Tower is a remarkable arms and armour museum, the Bowyer Tower has a collection of torture devices, the Beauchanp Tower's walls still show the carvings made by prisoners and the Bloody Tower is famous as the prison of Sir Walter Raleigh and the place where the Little Princes met their mysterious end.

Opening times: Weekdays all the year round, Sunday afternoons from March to October.
Telephone: 01-709 0765.

The Tower of London is often regarded as a sort of English Kremlin, a great fortress prison and a place where enemies of the Crown kept appointments with the executioner. What is not so widely realised is that for centuries it was also a palace. And in those days palaces needed to be strong enough to protect kings from their subjects. In 1078 William the Conqueror ordered work to be started on the Tower because of his well-placed distrust of London's 'fierce population', and nineteen years later, on the south-eastern corner of the city's Roman Wall, a rectangular keep of imported Caen stone was completed. In 1234 the castle was white-washed to improve its appearance by command of Henry III who had added the Great Hall, the Wakefield Tower and the gateway to the Bloody Tower. From then on more additions were made until it reached the eighteen-acre proportions with which we are familiar.

Not only is this ex-royal residence one of the world's most popular showplaces, it is the site of an amazing concentration of supernatural activity. One of its oldest ghosts is that of a bear, an animal which had once been housed in the Lion Tower. This building, as its name suggests, was a royal menagerie built by Edward I in 1278.

Had the poor creature been baited to death? If so his ghost is only one of the many Tower victims whose departure from life was anguished – kings, nobles and commoners have met violent, and sometimes secret, death within its walls.

When the gates are closed for the night, and the prophetic ravens sleep in their cage by the Lanthorn Tower, the time comes for the return of such restless blue-blooded phantoms as Edward V and his brother, Queen Anne Boleyn, Lady Jane Grey, Lord Northumberland, Lady Salisbury (who was chased round the block by the headsman) and Sir Walter Raleigh, together with spectres lower down the social scale such as Guy Fawkes. And there have been more mysterious manifestations.

'A most queer and utterly distasteful atmosphere' was how a Guards Officer described a sensation which overwhelmed him when he approached the Bloody Tower one night. It instilled him with such a sense of horror that his mind went blank and the next thing he knew he was hammering at the door of his mess three hundred yards away.

To me the most curious of the Tower's unusual materialisations was described in *Notes and Queries* for 1860 by Edmund Lenthal Swifte who had been appointed Keeper of the Crown Jewels in 1814, a post which he held for nearly forty years.

'One Saturday night in October 1817,' he wrote, 'I was at supper with my wife, our little boy and my sister-in-law, in the Jewel House, which then, comparatively modernised, is said to have been the doleful prison of Anne Boleyn and also of the ten bishops.

'The room was irregularly shaped, having three doors and two windows, which last are cut nearly nine feet deep into the outer wall. Between these is a chimney-piece projecting far into the room, which then was surmounted by a large oil picture.

'On the evening in question, the doors were all closed and dark cloth curtains were let down over the windows, the only light in the room being that from two candles placed on the table. I sat at the foot of the table, with my son on my right hand, his mother fronting the chimney-piece and her sister on the opposite side. I had offered a glass of wine and water to my wife, when on putting it to her lips she paused and exclaimed: "Good God! What is that?"

'I looked up and saw a cylindrical figure like a glass tube, seemingly about the thickness of my arm, hovering between the ceiling and the table. Its contents appeared to be a dense fluid, white and pale azure, like to the gathering of a summer cloud, and incessantly rolling and mingling within the cylinder.

'This lasted two minutes, when it began slowly to move before my sister-in-law; then following the oblong shape of the table, before my son and myself. Passing *behind* my wife, it paused for a moment over her right shoulder. (Observe, there was no mirror opposite to her in which she could then behold it.)

'Instantly she crouched down and with both hands covering her shoulder, she shrieked out: "Oh Christ! It has seized me!"

'Even now while writing, I feel the fresh horror of that moment. I caught up my chair, struck it at the wainscot behind her, then rushed upstairs to the other children's room and told the terrified nurse what I had seen. Meanwhile, the other domestics had hurried to the parlour, where their mistress recounted to them the scene, even as I was detailing it upstairs. The marvel, or as some will say the absurdity of all this, is enhanced by the fact that neither my sister-in-law nor my son beheld the apparition, though to their mortal vision it was as apparent as to my wife's and mine.

'On the next morning when I related the night's horrors to our chaplain after the service in the Tower church, he asked me: "Might not one person have his natural senses deceived? And if *one*, why not *two*?"

'My answer was, if *two*, why not two thousand? an argument which would reduce history, secular and sacred, to a fable.'

Another story connected with the Jewel House had a tragic ending. One midnight in January 1816, a sentry on guard outside it saw a figure like a huge bear appear at the door of the regalia room. Instinctively he raised his musket and lunged at the animal with his bayonet, with the result that the weapon passed through the spectral beast and the point of the bayonet dented the door. The bear advanced menacingly on the soldier who fainted on the stone floor. Other sentries ran to the spot and carried the unconscious man to the guard-room.

The next day Mr Swifte, who had then been Keeper only two years, visited the guard who was in bed with shock and wrote down his account of what had happened. Another sentry gave evidence that he had spoken to the victim just before the alarm had been raised, and that he had been alert and sober. Mr Swifte recorded: 'I saw him once again on the following day, but changed beyond my recognition, in another day or two the brave and steady soldier, who would have mounted a breach or led a forlorn hope with unshaken nerves, died at the presence of a shadow.'

Of the conventional spectres who haunt the Tower the best known is Anne Boleyn, whose ghost is also said to return to her old home of Hever Castle and to Blickling Hall in Norfolk. When she fell out of favour with Henry VIII and was escorted to the Tower she asked the Constable, 'Shall I go into a dungeon?'

'No, madam, you shall go into your lodging that you lay in at your coronation,' he replied.

When she entered the timber-framed house below the Bell Tower – known today as the Queen's House – the contrast in her first visit there must have struck her sadly. Soon afterwards in the Great Hall – which has since been demolished – she was charged with using spells to bewitch the king and committing adultery with her brother. Her own uncle, the Duke of Norfolk, pronounced her guilty and therefore should be burned at the stake or beheaded.

On 19 May 1536 she was led out to Tower Green before a congregation of nobles and aldermen of London. With remarkable composure she stepped on to the scaffold, made a brief speech and then knelt so that the executioner could strike off her head with a sword. The headsman had been brought over specially from Calais as this type of execution was a French custom which until then had not been practised in England. Sir William Kingston, the Constable of the Tower, was so moved by her courage that he wrote: 'This lady has much joy and pleasure in death.'

Anne's body was interred in the Tower church of St Peter ad Vincula, and it is to this gloomy shrine that her spirit is said to return. This chapel, whose name means 'St Peter in Chains', was used for burying the most important of the Tower's victims. When Queen Victoria took an interest in it the floor was taken up so that the human remains there could be identified and if necessary accorded a proper burial. Over two hundred were disinterred, but very few could be named.

A typical story concerning the church relates to an officer who was making a tour of inspection one night when he saw a light behind its clear windows. He asked a sentry what was the cause of the illumination, but the soldier replied that he had no idea although it was not unusual to see it.

The officer was curious enough to have a ladder brought which was propped up against the wall, the building being locked. When he climbed up and looked through the window he saw a number of people in old-fashioned costumes walking in mournful procession down the aisle, following a woman who, although her head was turned away, reminded him of portraits he had seen of Anne Boleyn. This ghostly promenade continued for another minute or so, then the figures dissolved and darkness returned to the silent church.

Another spot within the Tower grounds haunted by the tragic queen is Tower Green. She was one of only seven prisoners permitted to be executed there instead of providing a bloody show for the London rabble on Tower Hill. It was her appearance which caused a soldier of the King's Royal Rifle Corps to faint one night in 1864. He was found unconscious near his sentry box close to what used to be known as the King's House, and he was immediately put on a charge, for a sentry to be asleep at his post is one of the most serious military crimes.

In his evidence to the court martial he described how he had seen a white figure approach out of the darkness. Having shouted a challenge the prescribed three times, he raised his rifle as the figure continued to advance but before he could take any further action he saw that it was a headless woman. The shock was so great that he collapsed. Two other witnesses gave evidence supporting his statement, with the result that he was acquitted.

Another ghost who returns to her place of execution is the

pathetic shade of Lady Jane Grey who, at the age of fifteen, became Queen of England – not for a day as the mnemonic states, but for ten. She was last reported being seen in 1957.

Two other sad spectres are those of young Edward V and his brother Richard, the famous 'Princes in the Tower', who over the past five hundred years have been glimpsed in the Bloody Tower. It has been the popular and official belief that they were done to death here on the order of their wicked uncle the enigmatic Richard III, but more and more doubt is being cast on Richard's role as a murderer. It is now recognised that the Tudor writers – Shakespeare prominently among them – vied with each other to defame the last Plantagenet king for the benefit of the dynasty which replaced his house. Yet the only evidence against Richard was put forward verbally by Henry VII nineteen years after he had usurped Richard's throne. If the brothers had died as he claimed, why did he not announce the fact immediately after the Battle of Bosworth when he desperately needed to make Richard appear a villain as justification for his lawless seizing of the throne?

The real fate of the princes, and the case for their uncle's innocence, make an intriguing study but the two ghosts who have been seen side by side in the Tower give no hint as to the solution of one of the darkest of English historical mysteries.

Merseyside

SPEKE HALL
(Map reference: 78)

Seven miles from Liverpool's city centre, very close to Speke Airport, stands this large timber-framed house. Most of it was built between the 15th and 16th centuries, though the estate in which it is set goes back to the 12th century. Like other Tudor houses in the north-west, the walls of Speke Hall are beautifully patterned in black and white. Inside, there is interesting panelling, carving and plasterwork and some good oak furniture.

Opening times: Weekdays, Bank Holidays and Sunday afternoons the year round.
Telephone: Liverpool 427 7231.

A story worthy of a Victorian melodrama is often quoted to explain the ghost of Speke Hall. She is said to be a member of the Beauclerk family which inherited the house in 1736. One day her husband – described as either Lord Sydney Beauclerk or his son Topham Beauclerk – arrived with the news that he had been wiped out financially. His wife's sudden loss of security was such a shock that her mind gave way. She hurled her baby through the window. It died in the moat, after which its distraught mother committed suicide in the Great Hall.

Legend says that the baby was thrown from the window in the Tapestry Room, and this is certainly the hall's haunted apartment, but it seems that the story has no foundation because although the Beauclerks owned Speke Hall they never resided there.

Whatever the identity of the ghost, there is no doubt about her appearances in the Tapestry Room. On one occasion she materialised in a bedroom and then faded into the wall. When the area of the wall where she had vanished was investigated it was found that there was a forgotten secret passage behind it.

Norfolk

BLICKLING HALL
(Map reference: 11)

On the B1345 north-west of Aylsham, which is fifteen miles north of Norwich, Blickling Hall has been described as satisfying 'the most romantic conception of an English Country House'. This Jacobean mansion was built in the early part of the 17th century for Sir Henry Hobart, its dimensions being fixed by those of an earlier house which had stood on the same site.

Over the years a certain amount of rebuilding has been carried out, for example most of the panelling dates from the middle of last century. Among the hall's treasures is the decorated plaster ceiling in the long gallery and the Peter the Great Room with its fine Russian tapestry. Outside, the formal grounds and park, based on the 17th-century plan, have something to offer in each season. The house is in the care of The National Trust.

> *Opening times:* Daily from 1 April to 11 October except for Mondays and Fridays. Afternoons only from April to 21 May, and with late morning opening from 23 May to the end of September.
> *Telephone:* Aylsham 3471.

A ghost which appears in at least four different places in England is that of Anne Boleyn. As described in another part of this book she has been seen at Hever Castle crossing a bridge which spans the River Eden in the castle grounds. She has also been reported within the precincts of the Tower of London and at Bollin Hall in Cheshire which claims to be her birthplace. But it would seem that Blickling Hall in Norfolk is the setting for her most dramatic manifestation which traditionally takes place on the anniversary of her execution.

She has been seen to ride in a coach drawn by four headless horses up the avenue to the main door in the lovely old red-brick house. Here queen and equipage vanish.

According to some accounts the coachman is headless and so is the queen within the spectral vehicle. The apparition was first reported when the news was carried to Norfolk of the execution of Anne and Lord Rochfort with whom she was accused of committing incest. Then, four headless horses were seen galloping across the countryside dragging the corpse of a decapitated man behind them, obviously Anne's unfortunate brother. Since then her apparition has been more sedate with the carriage ride up to the door of the Hall.

The folklorist Christina Hole wrote just prior to the Second World War: 'The occupants of the house are so used to her annual appearance that they take little notice of her.'

CAISTER CASTLE
(Map reference: 14)

One mile west of Caister on Sea, on the A1064, rises the great tower of Caister Castle. One of England's first castles to be constructed of brick, it was built in the middle of the 15th century by Sir John Fastolfe whose name and nature were altered by William Shakespeare into one of his best known characters. In reality Sir John was a highly successful soldier who brought back from the Continent the idea of Caister being protected by elaborate water defences.

One of the castle's most popular aspects is its motor museum (which includes trams as well as motor cars), while those with nostalgia for the old Battersea Fun Fair will find its tree walk has been transferred to the grounds.

Opening times: Daily apart from Saturdays from 11 May to September.
Telephone: Wymondham 251.

It was a menacing harbinger which used to strike terror to the owners of Caister Castle. They knew that death was close to a member of the family when a huge old coach, unpleasantly like a horse-drawn hearse, swayed up to the castle as fast as the headless driver could urge his horses. After passing through the gates as though they were not there, it would circle the courtyard several times before vanishing in the direction from which it had come.

When the Paston family – the authors of the Paston Letters – inherited the castle in 1459 they also inherited the prophetic coach.

One of the Pastons defended the castle against the Duke of Norfolk during the Wars of the Roses in 1469, there being thirty defenders facing an army of 3000. In fear, Margaret Paston wrote to another son in London: 'Your brother and his fellowship stand in great jeopardy at Caister . . . Daubeney and Berney be dead, and divers other be greatly hurt, and they fail gun-powder and arrows and the place is sore broken by guns.'

Yet even with Norfolk's men outnumbering Paston's by a hundred to one, the duke still had to bring up reinforcements before Caister fell. When Norfolk died seven years later the Pastons reoccupied the castle, and once more the black coach would appear mysteriously before a family death.

The local Caister church is also haunted, the ghost being a monk who enjoys playing the organ. At the beginning of 1967 the vicar left a tape-recorder running through the night, and when he played it back next morning there was the sound of organ music on the tape.

FELBRIGG HALL
(Map reference: 34)

The hall, two miles south-west of Cromer on the A148, is a Jacobean house built in 1620 on the site of an earlier building. It is surrounded by a well-wooded park and its attractions include fine examples of rococo plasterwork, an 18th-century library containing books once owned by Dr Johnson and an orangery also from the 18th century. The house is in the care of The National Trust.

> *Opening times:* Tuesday, Wednesday, Thursday, Saturday and Sunday afternoons from 1 April to 11 October. Also Bank Holiday Mondays.
> *Telephone:* West Runton 444.

The ghost of Felbrigg Hall is a previous owner and a whaler, William Windham. He materialises in the Gothic-style library where he appears to be browsing through the books which he loved during his lifetime. It is an appropriate place for him to appear as he was responsible for the addition of the west side of the house and the library.

HOUGHTON HALL
(Map reference: 49)

The hall, which lies at Houghton thirteen miles east of King's Lynn, was built by Sir Robert Walpole. It has been described as the 'most complete and sumptuous Palladian house in England' and is full of architectural and decorative treasures. Of extra interest to visitors is the model soldier collection and different breeds of heavy horses to be seen in the stables.

> *Opening times:* Thursdays, and Bank Holidays and Sunday afternoons from 19 April to 27 September.
> *Telephone:* East Rudham 247.

Houghton Hall is believed to be haunted by the Brown Lady who also revisits nearby Raynham Hall. There is a story that when the Prince Regent was staying at the hall he awoke one night to see the phantom regarding him. Instead of being flattered that a lady ghost should take an interest in him, he was greatly upset and declared, 'I will not pass another hour in this accursed house for this night I have seen that which I hope to God I may never see again.'

It was at Raynham Hall that Captain Marryat, the Victorian author of sea stories, had a dramatic encounter with the Brown Lady. He asked his host, Lord Townshend, if he could sleep in the haunted room in which hung a portrait of the Brown Lady who in life was Dorothy Walpole, the sister of the famous Sir Robert. The captain was just about to go to bed when two young men came to tell him about a gun they would be using the next day. He said he would be interested to see it and went with them to their room.

After a short while he returned along a passage, accompanied by his friend who laughingly declared they would protect him from the house's famous phantom. Suddenly, they were aware of a lady coming down the corridor, and as they were in their nightshirts they stood behind a half-closed door.

As the figure came closer Captain Marryat realised her features were familiar – it was the face of Dorothy Walpole. In her hand was a lamp which clearly showed the brown material of her dress. As she came abreast of the three men she looked at them 'in such a diabolical manner' that their blood seemed to run cold.

The captain raised the gun. He squeezed the trigger and the shot went right through the Brown Lady without seeming to affect her – it was later removed from a door.

Captain Marryat was only one of many to see the ghost who later became the subject of a photograph taken by a couple of *Country Life* photographers, and experts who have examined the negative have been unable to discover the slightest suggestion of faking.

The Brown Lady's tragic story is that she was the daughter of Sir Robert Walpole, the Member of Parliament for Haughton in Norfolk. He was the guardian of Viscount Charles Townshend, but when Dorothy and he fell in love the old man refused permission for them to marry. His argument was that he did not want it to appear that he was gaining an advantage by marrying his daughter to his ward.

The viscount found another bride but became a widower in 1711 and not long afterwards he was married to Dorothy. At the time of the wedding he was unaware that in the meantime her lover had been the notorious Lord Wharton whose debts finally forced him to flee the country. Later on, when Townshend learned the truth, he was so enraged that he kept her a prisoner in her apartments. She died in 1726, officially from smallpox but many believed it was the result of a broken heart. It is said that her ghost returns to seek the children she was parted from when her husband discovered the secret of her past affair and treated her so unfairly.

Northamptonshire

ALTHORP

(Map reference: 3)

Standing off the A428 six miles north-west of Northampton, the house goes back to 1508 when it was built by Sir John Spencer. Its appearance was altered in the middle of the 16th century by Anthony Ellis, and again towards the end of the 18th when Henry Holland gave it its present appearance. It is a Mecca for art lovers as it houses one of the finest private art collections in Britain, begun by Robert, second Earl of Sunderland, three centuries ago. Portraits by Reynolds and Gainsborough are to be found in the Marlborough Room, while there are paintings by Van Dyck in the picture gallery.

> *Opening times:* Weekdays, Saturday afternoons except during May, June and July; Tuesday and Thursday afternoons from Easter to September; Thursday afternoons only during October, November and December. Sunday afternoon all the year round. The pleasure grounds are open on Saturday afternoons all the year round.
> *Telephone:* East Haddon 209.

Britain's most conscientious phantom is the groom who has materialised to carry out an important task at Althorp. According to expert writer on ghostlore, Christina Hole, he was seen by a certain Mr Drury when he was a guest at the house. Mr Drury, who later became an archdeacon, had stayed up late playing billiards with Lord Lyttelton. Then, as the two men finished their last game, a servant came and warned them to be very careful with the lights in their rooms as their host, Earl Spencer, had a phobia about fire.

In his room Mr Drury checked to make sure that there was nothing smouldering out of respect to the earl's wishes, and then went to sleep. He awoke some time later with the beam of a lantern playing on his face, and starting up, beheld a man in a striped shirt and cap observing him from the foot of the bed.

Naturally, he asked for an explanation but the man made no answer. This annoyed the future archdeacon and he declared angrily that this nocturnal visit would be reported to the earl next morning. Without a word the intruder turned and seemed to disappear into the dressing-room. This puzzled the guest because as far as he knew there was no other exit from the small chamber.

The next day he related his experience to Lady Lyttelton, the daughter of his host, and added that the only possible explanation could be that the fellow was drunk. She shook her head, and told Mr Drury that he had seen a ghost, in fact the spectre of a groom who had died two weeks earlier. It had been his duty each night to make the rounds of the house to see that no lights had been left burning, and that guests had not fallen asleep with candles unextinguished. The earl had given him orders to enter any room where he thought this might have happened.

Since then the faithful servant has appeared to other visitors whose lights burned late in order to ensure the safety of the house

Northumberland

ALNWICK CASTLE
(Map reference: 2)

Situated on the outskirts of the old-worldly town of Alnwick, the castle is owned by the descendants of the great Percy family who in the turbulent past regarded it as one of their most important strongholds. Its story goes back to the Norman Conquest when Gilbert de Tesson, who had been Duke William's standard bearer at the Battle of Hastings, became the first Norman master of Alnwick. After he rebelled against William Rufus, the site passed to Yvo de Vescy who began to build a fortification there to protect the countryside from Scottish reivers.

The present castle was begun by his son-in-law Eustace Fitzjohn in 1140. It was besieged by the Scots on several occasions, and by Henry IV in 1405 when Henry Percy was forced to surrender after rebelling against him. Later that century it was attacked during the Wars of the Roses but it escaped the attention of both sides during the Civil War because of its owners' masterly neutral policy.

After the Middle Ages it became run down as the use of artillery ended the military role of castles. But in 1755 the first Duke of Northumberland commissioned Robert Adam to restore it, and to him it owes its Gothic appearance and lead statues on the battlements which are such a striking feature today. A century later more restoration work was undertaken by Anthony Salvin, the Victorian architect who specialised in 'medievalising' castles which had lost their original appearance as successions of owners had sacrificed atmosphere for comfort. Salvin not only made the castle look like a fortress once more but also turned its interior into a replica of an Italian Renaissance Palace.

Today, over 80,000 members of the public visit Alnwick Castle annually, to view its treasures which include two Titians, and marvel at its decorated ceilings, particularly that of the dining room which was inspired by the ceiling of San Lorenzo in Rome.

Opening times: Afternoons from 3 May to 25 September excluding Saturdays.
Telephone: Alnwick 602722.

If a castle deserves to be haunted it is Alnwick, for down its history nine of its lords have died by violence or in mysterious circumstances. Yet it was not a spectral knight or warrior wraith which terrified those who lived under the shadow of its towers – it was a vampire.

Mercifully Britain has escaped the terror of the 'vampire epidemics' which from time to time swept Europe like a plague, and it is an interesting point that outbreaks of plague were often attributed to these horrific creatures. The dictionary definition of a vampire is a 'ghost or reanimated corpse that sucks blood of sleeping persons'.

Belief in them is so universal that I cannot help but believe that some grain of terrible truth lies behind the tradition. Legends of the 'undead' range from France to Asiatic Russia, from Japan to Africa. Even on remote islands in the Pacific Ocean the Talamaur is feared – a being which steals life from the dying. Vampires were known to the Greeks and Romans as *lamiae*, and before that they were mentioned in the writings of the ancient Chinese and Egyptians.

While the fear inspired by vampires is almost global, the habits of these monsters varies from country to country. In Ireland the vampire was called a Dreag-dul and it could only be stopped from its foul activities by building a great cairn of rocks on its grave, obviously to hold it down. In Serbia the remedy is far more bizarre and involves cutting off the vampire's thumbs and toes, hammering a nail into the neck and a sharpened hawthorn stick into the navel and soaking its hair with tow which is ignited by candles used during a deathbed vigil.

If Britain has lacked real vampires, at least her tradition of fictional ones makes up for it, and it is this tradition which has coloured our view of these creatures. This goes back to 1819 when a bestselling horror novel introduced the aristocratic vampire Lord Ruthven. At first this archetypal character was believed to have been a product of Lord Byron's pen – in fact the book was the work of his doctor, John Polidori. With Byron he attended a party where the guests each agreed to write a horror story. It must have been an inspired evening because another guest wrote a

103

novel whose title has become a household word – her name was Mary Shelley and her book *Frankenstein or the Modern Prometheus*.

Bram Stoker's *Dracula*, published in 1897, quickly eclipsed Lord Ruthven's popularity, and, along with Mary Shelley's monster, became the greatest inspiration for horror tales and movies ever since.

I have only been able to find three accounts of vampirism in the whole of Britain's extraordinary store of folklore. One occurred just over a hundred years ago at Croglin Low Hall in Cumbria, the others go very much further back, one relating to Melrose Abbey in Scotland and the other to Alnwick Castle.

In his *Historia Rerum Anglicarum*, William of Newburgh, the chronicler who lived between 1135 and 1200, described how a deceased master of the castle – 'a stranger to God's race and whose crimes were many' – would rise from his tomb during the hours of darkness to prowl the streets of the sleeping town.

The local priest told the historian how his body left such a stench of death and corruption behind him that pestilence broke out and many citizens fled from Alnwick to try and escape the fate overtaking so many of their neighbours. A group of men, blaming the vampire for the plague, banded together to rid themselves of the menace.

In Newburgh Priory, William wrote: 'They armed themselves, therefore, with sharp spades and betaking themselves to the cemetery, they began to dig. And whilst they yet thought they would have to dig much deeper, suddenly they came upon the body covered with but a thin layer of earth. It was gorged and swollen with a frightful corpulence . . .'

One of the men struck the bloated body with the edge of his spade and from the wound came a gush of fresh blood, proving that it was indeed a vampire. Immediately the corpse of the erstwhile master of the castle was taken beyond the precincts of Alnwick and burned to ashes. After this the pestilence subsided.

BAMBURGH CASTLE
(Map reference: 6)

Looming over sand dunes and a pale golden shore, Bamburgh Castle is situated by the village of the same name sixteen miles north of Alnwick. It has a story-book atmosphere, thanks to the restoration work commissioned by Lord Armstrong, of the Vickers Armstrong Company, and it has often been used as a setting for films.

Bamburgh has been a stronghold since Celtic times when it was held by the Votadini tribe, after which it was occupied by the Romans. After their departure it became the capital of Berniccia under the Saxon Ida. His grandson King Ethelfrith married Queen Bebba and the stronghold became known as Bebbanburgh, which evolved into Bamburgh.

It has seen the whole spectrum of English history – the setting up of Aidan's monastery on nearby Lindisfarne, the Viking raids of the 9th century and rebellion against William II. The Scots besieged it during the unhappy reign of King Stephen, breaching a wall and putting over a hundred of the defenders to the claymore. During the reign of King John, the castellan had a profitable sideline in piracy.

After the Wars of the Roses the castle deteriorated, and at the beginning of the 18th century it passed into the ownership of the Crewe family, one of whom was a Jacobite who hid in the castle's cellars when agents of George I sought him. His name was Tom Forster and in the Rebellion of 1715 he became 'The Pretender's General'. His sister, who engineered his escape from prison in London after the defeat of the Jacobites, is the Dorothy Forster who haunts the Lord Crewe Arms in the village of Blanchland.

Today visitors find the most fascinating feature in the castle the King's Hall which is like a film set for a historical drama, and also of interest there are collections of arms and armour, china and tapestries, but the main attraction is the majestic castle itself and its rampart views of the North Sea.

Opening times: Afternoons from 1 April to 31 October.
Telephone: Bamburgh 208.

As one might expect, the ghost of Bamburgh Castle is a knight who appears in the huge 12th-century keep. Those who have seen the apparition describe it as 'grey and indistinct' but the fact he is wearing armour is borne out by the clash of metal. Such a figure is in keeping with the castle which has the tradition of being Sir Lancelot's Joyous Gard, once the refuge for Tristram and Iseult and later for Queen Guinevere following her rescue from the stake at Carlisle Castle.

During the rebellion against William Rufus, its lord, Robert de Mowbray, Earl of Northumberland, was captured when the castle was attacked by royal troops. King William took the fettered prisoner before the battlements and sent a message to the earl's lady, that unless she had the gates opened she would see her husband's eyes gouged out. Bamburgh surrendered.

In the siege of 1464 Edward IV was so distressed to see artillery used on such a fine fortress that he warned the Lancastrian defenders that for every shot fired one of them would pay with his head. In June of that year, after the Red Rose was defeated at the Battle of Hexham, Bamburgh became the first English castle to surrender to gunpowder.

After this Bamburgh was allowed to deteriorate. Much later it was handed over to a charity run by Dr John Sharp, the curate of the village of Bamburgh who, having seen so many ships wrecked off the treacherous coast, started a lifeboat service. But the most spectacular rescue which took place before its ancient walls occurred in 1838 when Grace Darling and her father rowed through a storm from the lighthouse on the Farne Islands to rescue survivors from the wrecked steamship *Forfarshire*. If you visit Bamburgh, it is well worth visiting the Grace Darling Museum in the little town.

For students of folklore the legend of the Laidley Worm of Spindlestone Heugh – the Spindlestone being a natural tower of rock rising close to the castle's ramparts – is of more interest than the spectral knight, the word worm, or wyrm, being Old English for a dragon. The story of Bamburgh's enchanted dragon is told in an old painting on display in the castle. It tells how long ago an elderly widowed king of Northumbria married 'a dark woman of the wild land in the West'.

To ensure a welcome for his bride, the king sent a messenger ahead to Bamburgh to organise a splendid feast. As the royal cavalcade reached the castle, the main gate swung open and

Margaret, the king's eighteen-year-old daughter, ran out to kiss her father and meet her new stepmother.

'The Queen greeted her with kisses and a smiling face,' says the lettering on the painting. 'But she was really jealous of her Beauty and soon determined to be rid of so dangerous a rival.'

She invited the princess to her chamber to see some jewellery but once the girl was in the room the dark woman bewitched her into a horrible dragon-like creature which fled wailing from the castle.

The unwilling dragon made her lair among the crags by Spindlestone Heugh and, unable to control her new nature, became the plague of the district by carrying off livestock to devour. The fame of the Laidley Worm, as the dragon was called, reached a knight known as Childe Wynd – 'childe' then meaning a youth of noble birth. With his companions he sailed to Bamburgh, but the dragon was waiting for them on the shore. Her fiery breath prevented them from beaching their craft so they sailed on to Budle Bay where they were able to land safely.

The worm now retreated and Childe Wynd out-distanced his men as he overtook the beast among the Spindlestone crags. Raising his sword in the approved St George style, he just managed to stay his arm when tears began to flow down the dragon's reptilian face. Returning his blade to its scabbard, the knight listened while the Laidley Worm recounted her story and explained that the enchantment could be reversed if he would kiss her on the face three times before the sun set behind the castle.

Summoning up all his courage, Childe Wynd walked up to the creature and managed to do as he was asked. The bright scales of the dragon dimmed, the gigantic body shrank and the knight had to jump back as it exploded into flame. When the smoke blew away he saw a beautiful girl standing on the ashes of her former self. The young man wrapped her in his cloak and took her to Bamburgh where the old king was delighted by the ending of the Laidley Worm's predacity – and the return of his daughter. In fairy-tale tradition he offered Princess Margaret in marriage to the knight who had freed her from her enchantment.

Because Childe Wynd had broken the spell, it rebounded against she who had cast it – and the 'dark woman from the wild land in the West' was magically transformed into a speckled toad.

An old Bamburgh legend tells that she squats in a cavern

beneath the castle's foundations but, as with the Laidley Worm, it is still possible for the enchantment to be removed. Once every seven years the door of the cavern opens in case a hero wants to prove his bravery. All he would have to do is enter the dismal cave, unsheath Childe Wynd's sword, blow his horn thrice and then press the toad to his lips.

CALLAY CASTLE
(Map reference: 15)

Eight miles west of Alnwick lies Callay Castle surrounded by ancient, dreaming woods. What the visitor finds in this affectionately preserved estate is a 16th-century house built on to a 13th-century pele tower. Its showpiece is the drawing room which goes back just over two centuries and boasts amazing plasterwork. In the ballroom – which, like the drawing room, is two storeys high – there are rare tapestries from France showing a royal romance. The castle has attracted television teams not only from Britain but the USA.

Opening times: Saturday and Sunday afternoons from 2 May to 27 September, also on Bank Holidays.
Telephone: Whittingham 663.

An unusual occurrence actually affected the building of Callay Castle. When the first castle was started by the Clavering family in the reign of Henry II on the north bank of a small river which runs into the River Aln there was a mysterious interference. At the end of each day the masons would see their work collapse, while a voice boomed:

> *Callay Castle stands on a height,*
> *Up in the day and down in the night,*
> *Set it up on the shepherd's straw,*
> *Then it will stand and fall no more.*

The builders took the disembodied advice and began work on a new castle south of the river on a site known as Castle Hill. The foundations of the unfinished castle are still to be seen.

The second castle was later to have uncanny noises of its own. At the turn of the century, a Northumbrian correspondent of

108

W. T. Stead, the famous journalist, told how he had visited the castle with the local Society of Antiquities, the castle being the seat of Major A. H. Browne. Mrs Browne told him that in the older part of the castle, which had been the Claverings' pele tower, there was a room with a walled doorway. While Major Browne was on a holiday in India she took the opportunity to have the brickwork removed and found the room to be empty. She was convinced that in opening the sealed room she had allowed a ghost known as the Wicked Priest to escape, for ever since there have been strange noises echoing through the castle.

'Sometimes they are so loud you would think the house was being blown down,' she declared. 'There are tramplings along the passages and noises in some of the bedrooms.'

Mr Stead's correspondent concluded: 'Mrs Browne showed me the chamber, which was close to the roof. Probably it was one of those priest's hiding holes of post-Reformation times.'

CRASTER TOWER
(Map reference: 25)

Standing on the edge of the old fishing village of the same name, Craster Tower was originally a pele tower built in the 14th century, the house being added to it in the 18th.

Visiting by written appointment only.

Craster Tower has a strange and ancient reputation for being haunted, not only by phantoms but by a noisy entity which, it used to be said, boded ill for the head of the family if heard during the hours of darkness though it does not seem to have affected the present owner.

The Tower's most straightforward ghosts are the duellists and the Grey Lady. The former go back over three centuries when, because of involvement in a Border feud, a member of the Craster family slew a foeman by a battlemented wall. The sounds of that fight have echoed down the ages, the ringing of iron upon iron being heard as the invisible combatants re-enact their duel until it stops abruptly with a horrible cry.

In his book *North Country Squire*, Sir John Craster relates how appearances of the Grey Lady were commonplace in the days when his sister was being taught by a governess. The lady became so used to hearing the rustle of the phantom's dress that she gave up opening the schoolroom door to look at her when she heard her going past.

'It seemed that some female in very heavy rustling skirts came in by the first-floor front landing window, went slowly towards the pele tower, and there vanished,' Sir John wrote.

On one night his sister was in her bedroom when she heard the sound of a horse-drawn carriage come up the drive and halt at the front door.

The girl ran to her window, expecting to see the vehicle in the bright moonlight but there was no sign of it or any horses. While she was gazing about in surprise she suddenly heard it start up again and rumble towards the stables while continuing to remain invisible.

Apart from experiencing inexplicable 'banging and thumps apparently coming from the wall dividing the front from the back libraries', Sir John had a curious experience before breakfast on a particular morning when the maid asked him to come into the dining-room. One of a pair of heavy china vases which normally stood on the mantelpiece had been broken nearly in half. The top half remained in place on the shelf, the lower half lay in the fender. A pile of soot was found behind the firescreen, and five yards away on a window seat was the sooty imprint of one naked human foot.

What made the affair more puzzling was that there was not the slightest trace of soot on the floor between the window seat and the fireplace, while all the windows were secure with their shutters closed.

DILSTON HALL
(Map reference: 29)

The ruins of the old castle, built close to the edge of a steep bank overhanging a stream called Devil's Water, is close to the railway crossing on the A69 between Hexham and Corbridge. There is some doubt as to when the original castle was built, but the tomb of one of its former lords, Sir Thomas de Devilstone, in Hexham Abbey church, is dated 1297. The present rectangular tower goes back to the 15th century.

Today the hall is an educational establishment but permission can be obtained at the office to visit the ruins and the chapel which is still intact.

Although the old part of Dilston Hall is now a picturesque shell, I have included it because – along with the Radiant Boy of Corby – the haunting which takes place there is one of the best known on the Border. The manifestation takes the form of a light shining from one of the upper windows, once a beacon to guide home Lord James, the third Earl of Derwentwater. The lamp is held by the ghost of his wife who returns from time to time to repeat a vigil she carried out happily in life – until Derwentwater made his final return, in a coffin and headless.

The present rectangular tower of Dilston dates back to the 15th century when the property passed into the hands of Sir Edward Radcliffe whose descendants, always loyal to the Stuart cause, temporarily lost their possessions during the time of Oliver Cromwell. With the Restoration the family regained their land and James II gave Francis Radcliffe the titles of Baron Dilston, Viscount Langley and Earl of Derwentwater.

It is his grandson, James, who concerns us. He succeeded to the title in 1705 at the age of seventeen, having been educated at the court of St Germain with the son of the exiled James following the Glorious Revolution of 1688. His mother was Lady Mary, the daughter of Charles II by Moll Davis.

The young earl proved to be very popular throughout the district. A Border ballad of the time described him thus:

> *O, Derwentwater's a bonnie lord,*
> *And golden is his hair,*
> *And glinting is his hawking eye,*
> *Wi' kind love dwelling there.*

Young Catholic Derwentwater struck up a friendship with Protestant Thomas Forster and his sister, Dorothy, who lived in Blanchland about eight miles to the south. A tradition says that they might have married if it had not been for the difference of their faiths. (Should you visit Blanchland you will find it is the gentle ghost of Dorothy Forster who haunts her old home, now the Lord Crewe Arms, and who is one of the most affectionately regarded ghosts in England.)

In 1712 the earl married a Catholic lady named Anna Webb.

Three years later Lord Derwentwater and his retainers joined the Jacobite rebels seeking to replace George I with James Stuart, the Old Pretender. The inexperienced Tom Forster became the 'Pretender's General', and under his leadership the Jacobites met defeat at Preston.

The earl was among the seven rebel lords captured, and was imprisoned in the Tower of London. He pleaded guilty when charged with treason at Westminster Hall and threw himself on the king's mercy. King George had no mercy and Lord Derwentwater was beheaded on Tower Hill on 24 February 1716, after making a heroic speech in which he reaffirmed his allegiance to the man he had proclaimed as James III.

Strange signs accompanied the execution – blood dripped from the spouts of Dilston Hall, corn from the local mill was stained a reddish hue, as was the Devil's Water which from that day ceased to be a prattling stream and took on the sombre appearance which it has retained to this day.

It took two weeks for the earl's body to be brought from London to the Chapel of St Mary Magdalene which stands close to the hall. As the procession bore the coffin on the last stage of its mournful journey there was such an unusually brilliant display of the Aurora Borealis that ever since it has been referred to in the district as the Derwentwater Lights, and which were believed to reappear on each anniversary of the earl's execution.

SEATON DELAVAL HALL
(Map reference: 74)

Situated between Seaton Delaval and Seaton Sluice, the hall is usually referred to as 'Sir John Vanbrugh's masterpiece'. This ex-playwright turned architect completed the present mansion in 1728 for Admiral George Delaval who had asked him to design it 'for the entertainment of our old age'. Sadly Vanbrugh did not live to see the completion of the work which was one of the great architectural feats of the 18th century. On several occasions the hall has been damaged by fire and subsequently restored, the last time being in 1959. Today collections of ceramics, portrait paintings and fine furniture are to be seen while medieval banquets are held in the Great Kitchen.

Opening times: Wednesday, Sunday and Bank Holiday Monday afternoons from May to September.
Telephone: Seaton Delaval 481759.

All that remains of the old castle of Seaton Delaval is the Norman chapel, and the displaced phantom which continues to haunt it. But the baroque mansion which replaced the original building had its own ghosts too, or rather ghostly echoes from a time in the late 18th century when Lord Delaval's house parties were the talk – and the scandal – of the North-East. They may have given the locals something to tut-tut about, but the historian William Hewitt, in his *Visits to Remarkable Places*, described how, during the parties, the estate 'became in truth a perfect fairyland of light and beauty and music'.

It was probably the high spirits of Lord Delaval's beautiful daughters which inspired rumours of all sorts of delightfully naughty goings-on. Their ingenious practical joking was described in this old account thus: 'Beds were suspended by pulleys over trapdoors, so that when the guests were tired after a carouse, and were just dropping asleep, they were rapidly let down into a cold bath, and awoke in consternation, finding themselves floundering in darkness and cold water. Another contrivance was that of partitions between sleeping rooms, which could suddenly be hoisted up to the ceiling by pulleys, so that when ladies and gentlemen were retiring, and had dropped all their finery of wigs and hoop petticoats, they were astonished to see the walls of their rooms disappear, and to find themselves in a miscellaneous assembly of the oddest and most embarrassing description.'

The family home had to be abandoned when Lord Delaval's wealth had come to an end, but there were supernatural reminders of the good old days. At nights music from an invisible band sometimes floated through the grounds, and in the great empty rooms of the house caretakers heard the tapping of ladies' heels on the polished floors.

The ancient chapel had the most eerie reputation. When it was securely locked 'leadenish blue' lights were seen at its windows, lights that came without any human agency. After midnight it was noticed that the trees which grew close around it appeared to take on new and sinister shapes. A headless dog was seen on several occasions crouching in the chapel, but its principal spectre is the lady holding a child in her arms.

113

She is believed to be the bride of one of the Delavals who failed to return from a military expedition. From the battlements of the old castle she vainly waited for him to return – a vigil which was not ended by death. And after the demolition and rebuilding of the house her phantom moved to the chapel where during her lifetime she had prayed for her husband's return, kneeling by the 14th-century effigies of a knight and his lady who, unlike her, had been allowed to enjoy their span together.

WALLINGTON HALL
(Map reference: 82)

Standing at Cambo twelve miles west of Morpeth on the B6342, Wallington Hall was built above the cellars of an earlier, medieval house for Sir William Blackett in 1688. Its interiors mostly go back to the middle of the 18th century, while the central hall was added in the 19th and was decorated by Ruskin and William Bell Scott. The park was laid out by Capability Brown in the 1760s. Wallington was the home of the Trevelyan family from 1777 to 1942 when it was given to The National Trust by Sir Charles Trevelyan.

> *Opening times:* Wednesday, Saturday and Sunday afternoons from 1 to 15 April and during October. From 17 April to the end of September the house is open daily on afternoons excluding Tuesdays. The grounds are open all the year round.
> *Telephone:* Scots Gap 283.

One of the most intriguing haunted houses I have visited is Wallington Hall – perhaps what makes it intriguing is that one does not expect to find such a place in the depths of the Northumbrian countryside.

I was told that the haunting takes on the sound of invisible birds' wings beating against the window panes and – far more sinister to me – the sound of heavy breathing. Unfortunately, no one seems to know the story behind this mysterious aspiration although it has been heard quite frequently. It may be connected with Sir John Fenwick, the last of his family line, who was executed in 1697 for planning an assassination attempt on

114

William III. The Fenwick family had long owned Wallington, building a Tudor house on to a medieval pele tower.

After Sir John had been executed, his famous horse White Sorrel was confiscated and used by the king until one day the horse stumbled on a molehill and threw William, who died of his injuries. Thus White Sorrel avenged his master. The way in which the king was killed gave rise to the famous Jacobite toast, 'To the little gentleman in black velvet'.

Whatever the reason for the phantom breathing of Wallington Hall, the place definitely has an atmosphere in keeping with the best traditions of haunted houses.

Nottinghamshire

NEWSTEAD ABBEY
(Map reference: 67)

Off the A52 eleven miles north of Nottingham, Newstead Abbey
still has part of the original priory which was made into a mansion
by Sir John Byron in 1540. In later years the place seems to have
decayed because it was described as 'a heap of rubbish' when it
was inherited in 1798 by Lord Byron the poet. Twenty years later
it had to be sold to Colonel Wildman who employed the architect
John Shaw to restore it. Although most of the exterior is his work,
there remains the original cloister within the building surrounded
by vaulted medieval chambers.

As one would expect, the abbey contains relics of Lord Byron.
Other attractions include a 17th-century plasterwork ceiling in
the saloon, and rooms furnished in a variety of styles. The large
gardens are very pleasant, as is the lake in front of the house
whose shores are guarded by mock redoubts.

> *Opening times:* Afternoons daily from Good Friday to
> 30 September, the park and gardens being open all the year
> round.
> *Telephone:* Blidworth 3557.

In 1818 the poet Byron had to sell his ancestral home to clear his
debts. It must have been a bitter time for him because Newstead
Abbey had belonged to his family since 1540 when it had been
taken from the Black Canons and became the property of Sir John
Byron.

Part of the original priory remains and the house is haunted by
four ghosts: the 16th-century John Byron, who was glimpsed
reading beneath his portrait; the Black Friar, whose appearances
signalled disaster for the family; and a White Lady said to be
Sophia Hyett, the daughter of a bookseller, who was infatuated
with the poet and who after death haunted the abbey wringing her
hands and lamenting, 'Alas, my Lord Byron'. The fourth ghost is
a phantom Newfoundland dog.

116

Byron claimed that he saw the ill-omened friar the night before his marriage to Anne Millbanks, but that might have been a piece of sardonic humour. The dog was Byron's beloved Bo'sun who was probably the most faithful companion the poet ever had. He was broken-hearted when Bo'sun died, and buried him in a grave where once the Black Canons' high altar stood. A memorial stone carries a poem dedicated to 'Boatswain, a Dog' which includes the well-known couplet:

> *'But the poor dog, in life the firmest friend,*
> *The first to welcome, foremost to defend.'*

Oxfordshire

HINTON MANOR
(Map reference: 48)

Hinton Manor, at Hinton Waldrist twelve miles west of Oxford, is surrounded by a moat which once protected a medieval castle. A Regicide's house, it was begun in the Elizabethan era and was added to in 1700, and again in 1830 when the present front of the house was built.

Visiting by written appointment only.

It is another of England's coloured lady ghosts which revisits Hinton Manor. White, Green and Grey Ladies are comparatively common; in this case the phantom is one of the rare Red Lady variety. Her name comes from the full-length wine-coloured dress she wears when she materialises in the music room where she plays the spinet.

When someone glimpses her she is said to smile at them in a friendly fashion, and she seems so substantial that frequently it is not realised she is a ghost until later.

A story told at Hinton concerns a lady house guest who followed the sweet sound of a spinet into the music room where she saw a lady playing. The guest hurried back to her husband and said accusingly, 'I wasn't told that it was formal dress this evening.'

He hastened to reassure her that it wasn't whereupon she informed him that she had already seen another woman in a long gown.

'In the music room?' he asked. When she nodded he told her – perhaps with a certain relish – that she had encountered the Hinton Ghost.

MINSTER LOVELL HALL
(Map reference: 62)

Designated an ancient monument, the ruins of Minster Lovell Hall are sited in the village of the same name near Witney. They go back to the first half of the 15th century when William, seventh Baron Lovell, built a manor house in a beautiful setting overlooking the River Windrush.

Henry VII took the house away from the Lovells following the Battle of Bosworth which ended the Wars of the Roses, and it went into the ownership of the Coke family. For a while it was the home of Thomas Coke, the first Earl of Leicester. Sadly the hall was abandoned and some of the buildings were partly demolished in the middle of the 18th century.

Opening times: Department of the Environment standard hours.

At the beginning of the 18th century workmen employed to renovate Minster Lovell Hall had a bizarre experience. Removing old slabs from a floor they found themselves gazing into a yawning black space. It was a vault which had been sealed up and forgotten. Such places inspire men with thoughts of treasure, and in this case a lantern was soon procured and lowered into the darkness.

But it was not gold coins which reflected the candle's feeble rays but the white bones of a skeleton. Nor was it a skeleton which had long ago been interred in some family vault – this skeleton was seated in a chair and sprawled across a table on which was some paper, a quill pen and a worm-eaten book.

The men remembered that Minster Lovell was haunted by a tall figure, and also by the sound of rustling paper which seemed to come out of the floor. Here, it seemed, was the reason for the haunting because these bones proved an old story connected with the house. Once it had been the home of the Lord Lovell who had supported the impostor Lambert Simnel. Following the battle of Stoke he became a fugitive and went into hiding in his own home. One loyal servant looked after his wants, taking food to him in the secret chamber which he left locked so that no one would find his master by accident. When the man died Lord Lovell starved to death, a prisoner in his own hiding place.

Today the ruins of Minster Lovell are still haunted. Groans and cries of lament are heard coming from the ground where the secret cellar was located.

Surrey

HAM HOUSE
(Map reference: 41)

This Jacobean residence, situated a mile south of Richmond on the bank of the Thames opposite Twickenham, was built in 1610 by Sir Thomas Vavasour, Knight Marshal to James I. Later it passed by marriage to the Duke of Lauderdale who was Charles II's minister in 1671. At this time it was redecorated in the extravagant style of the day by the architect William Samwell. Since then there have been hardly any alterations to the house or its contents, which means that its 17th-century rooms are almost unique. Charles II furnishings, a portrait gallery and formal garden add to the period atmosphere. The house is in the care of The National Trust and The Victoria and Albert Museum.

> *Opening times:* Afternoons, excepting Mondays, all the year round. Closed at Christmas and on Good Friday.
> *Telephone:* 01-940 1950.

One of London's most famous haunted sites is Ham House whose three separate manifestations go back to the reign of Charles II and one of which is the most delightful in the whole gamut of British ghostlore. The best known Ham phenomenon is a tapping which has echoed down through the centuries and which was originally made by an old lady's walking stick. She was the Duchess of Lauderdale who, as she grew older, tapped her way about the house – though why such a mundane activity should become invested with supernatural qualities no one can say. Although it was believed that hauntings were the result of human trauma, usually on the point of death, most hauntings are not the least dramatic and are quite inconsequential. If it was human emotion which caused images to be imprinted on some 'psychic tape' it is surprising that there are no reports of ghosts re-enacting their love-making.

The Thames towpath runs close to the house and it is here that a phantom in 'cavalier' dress has been seen. His story is that he was a royal messenger who visited Ham with King Charles and, in the course of a merry evening, drank too much wine with the result that he stumbled from the path and was drowned in the river.

The last and most endearing tale is that of a little King Charles spaniel who appears on the terrace at the rear of the house. As lively as any living dog, he has even been seen frisking in the daylight hours.

HAMPTON COURT PALACE
(Map reference: 42)

Although Hampton Court was never used by a monarch after the death of George II in 1760, the palace with its crenellated walls, turrets of time-mellowed brick and formal gardens overlooking the Thames is the most picturesque of England's royal residences.

Though many kings and queens have lived there, it is with Henry VIII that it is most closely associated. Built in his reign by Thomas Wolsey, Archbishop of York, it stands on a site he acquired in 1514, the year before he became a cardinal and the Lord Chancellor of England. The most powerful and richest of Henry's subjects, Wolsey made Hampton Court the symbol of his success. His household there numbered five thousand, and nearly three hundred furnished rooms were always kept in readiness for guests. It is recorded that when a treaty was signed between France and England in 1527, the Lord Chancellor entertained the French Ambassador and his retinue of four hundred in splendour there.

This magnificence was not to last for, in 1529, after losing favour with the king, he was stripped of his privileges and in a desperate bid to win back royal favour he presented Hampton Court and all its contents to Henry. This gesture did little good for on 30 October 1529 his lands were declared forfeit to the Crown and in 1530 he was arrested on a charge of high treason. He died while being brought down to London to stand trial. One can imagine the feeling with which he made his most famous remark just prior to his death: 'Had I but served God as diligently as I have served the King, he would not have given me over in my grey hairs.'

Delighted with his acquisition, Henry began to enlarge it and make it one of the most luxurious palaces in the kingdom. It was here he brought Anne Boleyn, Jane Seymour, Anne of Cleves, Catharine Howard and Katherine Parr, and later his three children were all to hold court there.

Henry VIII's efforts at enriching Hampton Court Palace were continued by William and Mary who commissioned Sir Christopher Wren to enlarge it in the classical style as an answer to Versailles. On Queen Mary's death in 1694 the work was halted. Only half of what had been planned had been carried out but as the improvements were also of brick, there was luckily no clash of styles.

Among the rooms open to the public are the state rooms which William designed for his patrons. Many paintings from the royal collection are on display.

Opening times: Department of the Environment standard hours.

One would expect that the foremost ghost to haunt Hampton Court would be that of Cardinal Wolsey grieving for his lost palace and yet there was no report of his phantom having been seen until 1966. During a *Son et Lumière* production at the palace the figure of Wolsey was noticed under one of the archways and at the moment of being seen was thought to be an actor. When it was realised that no actor was playing the part of the Cardinal, nor would have been in that position during the performance, the real identity of the figure was guessed.

The other ghost that one would expect to find there would be that of Henry himself, but the nearest I could find of anything supernatural relating to him was a vague story of irregular footsteps that suggested one leg dragging. (In later life Henry was to suffer with an ulcerated leg.) Such an insignificant haunting hardly befits a king who altered the whole course of English history and had such a traumatic personal life.

It was at Hampton Court that Henry's third wife, Jane Seymour, bore him a sickly son and then died seven days later. Dressed in white and carrying a candle, her phantom has been seen to glide from the old Queen's Apartments, through the Silver Stick gallery and down the stairs into the large Clock Court where, during the daytime, tourists enter through an archway named after her predecessor – Anne Boleyn's Gateway.

A much more dramatic royal ghost is that of Queen Catharine

Howard. In the same month that Anne of Cleves was divorced she became Henry's fifth queen, but in November of the following year, 1541, Archbishop Cranmer accused her of having had sexual relations with a relative, a musician, before she married Henry. On 13 February 1542 she was beheaded.

When she was arrested at the palace she managed to break free from her captors and run along a gallery – to this day known as the Haunted Gallery – to the chapel where Henry was at prayer. She beat on the door and screamed to her husband for mercy but Yeomen of the Guard seized her and she was dragged away, still screaming. Apparently Henry did not allow his wife's cries to interfere with his devotions. In the past her ghost has been seen and heard re-enacting this dreadful scene on the anniversary night of her arrest. Eye witnesses who have seen her have described her as a figure running with her long hair streaming behind her but who dissolves almost as soon as she is observed.

Another well-authenticated ghost of Hampton Court is that of Mistress Sybil Penn who was the foster mother of Henry's sickly son, Edward VI. Because of the devotion she had shown to the boy, she was given apartments at Hampton Court when he died at the age of sixteen. She died there of smallpox in 1562, and was interred at the old church of Hampton-on-Thames where an elaborate monument was erected, proving the esteem with which she had been regarded. A long poem extolling her virtues was carved on it, the first lines being:

Penn here is brought to home, the place of long abode
Where vertu guided hathe her shipp into the quyet rode
A myrror of her tyme, for vertues of the mynde
A Matrone suche as in her dayes the like was herd to find . . .

There was nothing to remind the world of Mistress Penn except this monument until 1829 when the church was pulled down and her grave desecrated, the memorial being moved into the lobby of the church which replaced it. Soon afterwards the ghost of Mistress Penn returned to the apartments at Hampton Court where she had lived so long ago. By now the rooms were occupied by a family called Ponsonby who reported hearing the sound of a woman's voice and the noise made by a spinning wheel which appeared to come through one of the walls. These sounds caused such interest that the Board of Works authorised a wall to be demolished and behind it was found a room which had been sealed up for centuries. Under the covering of dust was found a spinning wheel which it is possible was once used by Mistress Penn who, during her lifetime, had been noted for her spinning.

People unfamiliar with the Penn monument in Hampton Church described the ghost as wearing a long straight dress and a close-fitting headdress such as was fashionable with Tudor matrons – they could have been equally describing the effigy which laid with its hands pressed together in prayer on Mistress Penn's tomb. One witness who knew nothing of Mrs Penn was Princess Frederica of Hanover who, when she saw Hampton's Lady in Grey, gave a description identical to that of the effigy.

A little over a hundred years ago Lady Hildyard lived in grace-and-favour apartments overlooking Fountain Court, a beautiful colonnaded square in the heart of the State apartments. She was disturbed by the sight of two ghosts there, as well as by inexplicable tapping sounds. She complained to the Lord Chamberlain about the manifestations but nothing was done. It is easy to imagine her being regarded as a crank. Then, in 1871, when workmen were excavating in Fountain Court opposite her apartments, two skeletons were uncovered which were thought to be the remains of a couple of cavaliers from the time of the Civil War – Lord Francis Villiers and a friend who were killed in a skirmish with Roundheads.

Another version of the story suggests they were two soldiers from the time of William III, but no doubt Lady Hildyard felt some satisfaction at this vindication of her story.

Other Hampton Court ghosts include the White Lady who has been seen on the Thames bank where once the royal barges used to berth; the alleged phantom of Archbishop Laud who lost his head on Tower Hill in 1645 for 'endeavouring to subvert the laws, to overthrow the Protestant religion, to act as an enemy to Parliament'.

A party of unrecognised ghosts was seen late one night in February 1907 by a police constable with twenty years' experience in the Force.

'On this particular night,' he reported, 'I went on duty at the east front of the Palace at ten o'clock and had to remain there until six o'clock next morning. I was quite alone, and was standing close to the main gates, looking towards the Home Park, when suddenly I became conscious of a group of figures moving towards me along what is known as the Ditton Walk. It is a most unusual thing to see anyone in the garden at that time of night, but I thought it probable that some of the residents in the Palace had been to a party at Ditton, and were returning on foot. The party consisted of two gentlemen in evening dress and seven or nine ladies. There were no sounds except what resembled the rustling of dresses.

'When they reached a point about a dozen yards from me I turned round to open the gates to let them in. The party however altered their course and headed in the direction of the Flower Pot Gates, to the north of the gardens. At the same time there was a sudden movement amongst the group; they fell into processional order, two deep, with the gentlemen at the head. Then, to my utter amazement, the whole crowd of them vanished; melted, as it seemed to me, into thin air. All this happened within nine yards of where I was standing, the centre of the broad gravel walk in front of the Palace. I rushed to the spot, looking up and down, but could see nothing or hear nothing to explain the mystery.' And indeed the mystery has remained unexplained.

Sussex

ARUNDEL CASTLE
(Map reference: 4)

Halfway between Worthing and Chichester at the town of the same name Arundel Castle – the home of the Dukes of Norfolk and their ancestors for over seven centuries – is one of the show places of Britain. It has often been described as a Windsor Castle on a smaller scale, complete with a round keep, upper and lower baileys, and stone steps protected by battlemented walls leading up to the keep. What delights the tourists is that it is not a ruin requiring imagination to refurbish it, but it looks like an almost new Norman fortress. This is thanks to the restoration work of Henry, the fifteenth Duke of Norfolk, who rebuilt it as close to the original as possible. The work was begun in 1890 and finished thirteen years later at a cost of £600,000.

It is not only its romantic turrets and towers which are such an attraction, its interior gives it pride of place among stately homes. There is a glorious chapel dating back to 1380 (restored after being desecrated by Cromwell's troops), an exhibition of ceremonial robes of the various orders of chivalry – including those of the Dukes of Norfolk – and the uniform which the present Duke wears as Earl Marshal of England. In the armoury there is a fascinating collection of weapons and armour, including a huge sword called 'Mongley', which was a medieval two-handed tournament sword. There are also paintings by Gainsborough, Van Dyck and Holbein as well as furniture dating back to the 15th century.

> *Opening times:* During the summer months the castle is open during the afternoon from Sunday to Friday; and on Monday to Friday afternoons from 30 March to 17 April and from 7 September to 30 October. Not open on Saturdays.
> *Telephone:* Arundel 883136.

The story of Arundel Castle began during the reign of Edward the

Confessor although it was not until William I gave the fortress to his relative, Roger de Montgomery, that stone began to replace its timber construction. One of Roger's sons, Earl Robert, rebelled against Henry I who besieged the castle in 1102, and the fact that the castle was able to hold out for twelve weeks against the royal army indicated its strength.

When Henry I died, his queen Adela of Louvain retired there where she fell in love with William d'Albini. He was a supporter of the Empress Matilda in her fight against King Stephen in the chaotic years when, as a chronicler graphically put it, 'Christ and his saints slept'.

William d'Albini was known as 'William of the Strong Hand', and this nickname, together with the lion rampant on the Albini arms, is said to have originated when he was in Paris contending a tournament. He performed so well in the lists that the Queen Dowager of France made it clear that she would not be averse to him as a husband. He made it equally clear that he was already betrothed to the Queen Dowager of England. Feeling insulted, the French queen tricked d'Albini into entering a grotto in her palace garden where a hungry lion was waiting. But he rushed upon the animal, wrenched its jaws apart and pulled out its tongue.

After returning to England and marrying Adela he became the Earl of Arundel, and when the Empress Matilda arrived in England to claim the throne he allowed her to stay at Arundel Castle. King Stephen then surrounded the castle with his army and soon had the queen in his power,, but the king was too much of a gentleman for his own good. Many a monarch of those days would have seized this opportunity to remove his rival by the stroke of a headsman's axe, but Stephen merely gave her a safe conduct to Bristol and sent an escort of his own troops to protect her. She repaid this courtesy by joining with her half-brother Earl Robert against the king, and soon became the mistress of the west of England.

When her son, Henry II, became the first Plantagenet king of England, William d'Albini was rewarded for his services by being given command of the king's army in Normandy, and it was during this period that the round keep was built on the motte within the castle walls.

The Albini line died out in 1243, and the castle passed to the Fitzalan family. They held it until 1580 when the daughter of the last Earl of Arundel inherited the property with her husband

128

Thomas Howard, Duke of Norfolk, their family retaining the castle ever since.

In the Civil War Parliamentarian forces besieged Arundel for eighteen days, bombarding it with a cannon placed in the tower of St Nicholas's church. The marks of its cannonballs are still to be seen on the walls of the barbican towers.

Cromwell's artillery sounded the death knell for castles as places of military importance, and Arundel was allowed to remain a ruin until 1716 when the 8th Duke of Norfolk began to restore it. This work was carried on by his descendants until today Arundel stands in its former glory.

As one would expect it has its share of ghosts, including the silvery shape of a young girl sometimes seen in moonlight near one of the towers from which she threw herself as the result of an unhappy love affair.

Another ghost, the Blue Man, appears in the library bending over an old book. Dressed in a blue costume from the time of Charles II, he seems to be seeking some piece of information which he can never find.

In the kitchen, during the dead of night, there is sometimes heard the rattle of pots and pans – the sound of a scullion hard at work. It is a supernatural echo going back two centuries to when a kitchen lad was brutally treated there. From time to time a more impressive sound booms from the past, the thunder of the Parliamentarian artillery which pounded the castle walls during the Christmas siege of 1643.

It is an old Arundel belief that when one of the family is about to die, a strange white bird is observed fluttering desperately against the panes of one of the castle windows.

HERSTMONCEUX CASTLE
(Map reference: 46)

The castle, built by Sir Roger de Fiennes in the 15th century, looks like an illustration from an historical romance as it dreams above its reflection in a vast lake-like moat. Despite its atmosphere of ancient chivalry, the castle today has a space-age function. In 1948, when the lights of London and its polluted atmosphere were making astronomy impossible at Greenwich,

The Royal Observatory was moved to the cleaner air of Sussex and housed in the castle. The grounds are open to visitors.

It is a Phantom Drummer who haunts Herstmonceux Castle, and as if this is not enough in itself, let me add that he is said to be nine feet tall and the last time he beat a rataplan in life was on the field of Agincourt. This makes him one of our senior ghosts as the battle was fought in 1415. The drummer was in the retinue of Sir Roger de Fiennes, who built Herstmonceux, when he went over to France with Henry V's army. In the remarkable battle, which stunned Europe with the devastating effectiveness of archers against armour-plated knights, only 120 English soldiers were killed, while their firepower was responsible for the deaths of over eight thousand of the enemy. Among the English casualties was Sir Roger's drummer, and such was his loyalty to Herstmonceux that his shade returned to re-enact the drumming which had rolled across the battlefield.

That is one explanation, another is more prosaic. It has been suggested that the ghostly drumbeats were the work of a castle gardener who at midnight beat a drum to frighten away members of the family while smugglers hid contraband in the castle vaults. The idea is given weight by the fact that there is a room in the castle known as Drummer's Hall which was used by a French gardener but it seems unlikely that the owners of Herstmonceux could be fooled so easily. It is possible that drumming might have been used to keep superstitious villagers away while the smuggling went on but that would only be effective if a Phantom Drummer was already feared. Another point is that the Phantom Drummer is a very old tradition of the castle, spanning a much longer period than one man's lifetime.

There is another story that the drumbeats were made by a living person: an elderly owner of the castle became so religious that he decided to model his life on the early Christian hermits who hid themselves away from temptation. To this end, he retired to a small cell in the castle where he lived on bread and water, allowing the outside world to believe he was dead. But he was still worldly enough to want to keep suitors away from his young and beautiful wife, and at night he beat a drum on the castle ramparts in the hope that their fear of the drummer would dissuade them from nocturnal visits. Her ladyship had no wish to lead a hermit-like life like her old husband, so she locked the door of the recluse's cell and left him to starve to death. But the beat of the Phantom Drummer continued long after the religious fanatic had turned to dust in his hidden retreat.

Apart from the drummer, Herstmonceux has other spectres. In 1727, when part of the castle was in a ruinous condition, an heiress was also starved to death. To prevent her inheriting her rightful property the governess was bribed to lure her to a remote chamber and imprison her. The girl died of hunger on the eve of her twenty-first birthday, and since then her shade has been seen at the edge of the broad moat.

Augustus Hare wrote about the ghost of a sleep-walker who fell to his death from the ramparts and who still haunts the castle, slowly fading away when seen. Yet another phantom is that of a man with a pig-tail dressed in old-fashioned sailor's clothes.

The midnight appearance of four spectral huntsmen galloping in the vicinity of the estate goes back to 1541 when wild Lord Dacre, master of the castle at that time, suggested an unusual hunt to his companions, George Roydon, John Frowdys and John Mantell. He had quarrelled with a neighbour named Sir Nicholas Pelham and thought it would be a great joke to hunt his deer at night. When the moon was high enough, the reckless quartet galloped over the castle drawbridge and across the fields to the Pelham estate. Close to the Cuckmere river they met a gamekeeper with two companions who angrily ordered them off. When the trespassers answered his words with abuse he went for them with a staff.

The huntsmen unsheathed their swords — perhaps playfully at first, and the sound of steel striking hard wood rang through the woods until the gamekeeper fell mortally wounded.

Lord Dacre and his friends galloped off while the dying gamekeeper was carried home. He managed to tell Sir Nicholas that he had recognised his assailants. The other two men backed up his story, and when the victim died a couple of days later Lord Dacre and his friends were charged with murder. Being a noble he was housed in the Tower of London and tried by his peers but, like Roydon, Frowdys and Mantell, he was found guilty and sentenced to death.

There was argument over the verdict, many people believing

131

that the young lord was guilty of manslaughter rather than murder as the gamekeeper's death had been the result of a brawl and there had been no intent to kill.

Just before the execution it was believed that Henry VIII would grant a reprieve and a 16th-century historian wrote: 'On the 18th of June the sheriffs of London were ready at the Tower to receive the prisoner and lead him to execution on Tower Hill; but a gentleman of the Lord Chancellor's house came and in the King's name ordered a stay of execution until two in the afternoon, which caused many to think that the King would have granted him his pardon.'

But no further word came and Lord Dacre and his companions were executed. Meanwhile, according to tradition, the Phantom Drummer of Herstmonceux beat an eerie prelude to their deaths.

MICHELHAM PRIORY
(Map reference: 61)

Located seven miles north of Eastbourne on the B2108 just off the A22, this Augustinian priory was established in 1229, and is protected by one of England's largest moats. The buildings are arranged conventionally about a cloister, the present house being made up of part of this and a Tudor addition which was built after the Dissolution. Today Michelham offers the visitor tapestries and 17th-century furniture, a museum of local archaeology, exhibits from the Alice Mummery collection of early musical instruments and an interesting Doll's House. Outside there is a forge and a collection of old agricultural implements and farm vehicles. The priory is in the care of the Sussex Archaeological Trust.

Opening times: Daily from Good Friday to 18 October.
Telephone: Hailsham 844224.

After the Dissolution Michelham Priory became a farmhouse and its ghosts go back to that time. There is a Grey Lady who haunts the gatehouse, while in the Tudor Room in the priory a lady wearing Elizabethan dress has been seen. A very unusual phantom in a black cloak has also been observed descending diagonally from the ceiling to the floor opposite an inglenook

132

fireplace. It is thought that he follows the course of a staircase which was removed long ago. Another ghost was mentioned in a letter sent to me by John Akers, of Hampden Park, who wrote:

'A man I knew was at one time employed at Michelham Priory. One day he met a stranger, an American tourist, walking in the grounds. During conversation the American asked how many monks there were at Michelham nowadays. My friend replied that there had been none since the Dissolution in 1536. "Really," said the other, "then who was it who let me in this morning?"'

Tyne and Wear

WASHINGTON OLD HALL
(Map reference: 85)

Standing at Washington village six miles south of Newcastle, this Jacobean manor house incorporates parts of a 12th-century house which was the home of George Washington's ancestors from 1183 to 1613. The family took its name from here. In 1936 the house had become so neglected that it was scheduled for demolition but luckily it was restored with great care when it was given to The National Trust.

Today there is period furniture, Delftware and some Washington relics on display. In the garden is a tree which President Carter planted in 1977.

> *Opening times:* Saturday and Sunday afternoons from November to February, and daily afternoons, excluding Tuesdays, from March to October.
> *Telephone:* Washington 475037.

It would be nice if more was known about the phantom in a long grey dress who appears to float along an upstairs passage in Washington Old Hall. Then American tourists might have the satisfaction of visiting a place haunted by a female ancestor of their first President. But most ghosts seem to have no interest in the living – it is as though they are in a dimension of their own – and the enigmatic lady retains her secrets despite the fact that sightings of her have been more and more frequent over the last few years, perhaps in ratio to the increasing number of visitors to the hall.

Warwickshire

WARWICK CASTLE
(Map reference: 84)

Standing on a steep cliff above the River Avon in the centre of Warwick, Warwick Castle is one of the best inhabited castles in England. The original fortification on this site was built before the Norman Conquest by King Alfred's daughter Ethelfleda. The present castle goes back to the 14th century. Since then there have been additional building and alterations, the last being the work of Anthony Salvin in the 1860s.

In 1978 the Earl of Warwick sold the castle to Madame Tussaud's. For the visitor there are state rooms said to rival those of Windsor Castle, a collection of paintings by such masters as Rubens and Van Dyck, one of the best collections of armour in Britain and parkland which was landscaped by Capability Brown.

> *Opening times:* Open daily all the year round apart from Christmas Day.
> *Telephone:* Warwick 45421.

Warwick Castle is proud of the ghost of Sir Fulke Greville, not only is he mentioned in their literature but there is a taped version of the story playing at intervals in the haunted room.

Sir Fulke Greville, first Baron Brooke, was an Elizabethan poet who completed his education at Jesus College in Cambridge. He wrote over a hundred sonnets and a couple of tragedies, but his life was not that of a literary recluse for he also served as a Privy Councillor.

While in London in 1628, he was stabbed by an old and trusted servant named Ralph Heywood. Heywood committed suicide afterwards, but Sir Fulke lingered a month before death overtook him. Then his restless spirit returned to his castle which he had restored at great expense to 'the most princely seat within the midland parts of this realm', which is still a good description of Warwick.

The haunted room is Sir Fulke's study which is furnished just as it would have been when he sat there, quill in hand, before his parchment. His spectre still haunts it. Recently Mrs Joan Ryan heard an eldritch sound above the noise of her vacuum cleaner when she was cleaning the room. She described it as a loud 'raking sound' coming from the panelling on which hung a portrait of the murdered gentleman.

'I turned off the machine, and a few moments later I heard the same noise again,' she said. 'I was so frightened I could not even find the key to let myself out of the room. I had never believed in ghosts, but I do now.' After this she refused to work in the tower.

While I was visiting Warwick Castle a lady at the sales counter told me that the ghost of Sir Fulke had been seen in the castle shortly before my arrival.

In *Notes and Queries* Volume 14, 1918, I came across another story of Warwick Castle submitted by Mr J. Harvey Bloom who wrote:

An ancient dame had the privilege of selling spare milk (at the castle) and by a system not uncommon to modern milk vendors she so cheated her customers that the earl hearing of it cancelled the privilege. She then bewitched the castle, usually in the form of a black dog. The chaplain and the vicars of St Mary's and St Nicholas brought the evil one to rest by reading passages of scripture, and eventually followed the witch in the form of a dog to the height of Caesar's Tower from which she or it sprang into the stream to a chamber prepared under the milldam. Her statue was placed above the tower battlements until blown down some years back.

Warwick Castle is well worth visiting because it has everything a castle should have – from a defensive mound built by Ethelfleda, daughter of King Alfred, to a magnificent collection of armour in the Great Hall; and for those interested in the macabre there is a display of torture instruments, some of which are from the Nuremburg Castle collection, in the dungeon.

Wiltshire

LITTLECOTE HOUSE
(Map reference: 56)

Off the A4 three miles west of Hungerford, this historic brick and flint manor goes back to the 15th century. The first family to own the house was the Darrells, and in 1589 it passed to the Pophams who later supported the Parliamentarian side in the Civil War. As a reminder of those days, Roundhead arms and uniforms are displayed on the walls of the splendid Great Hall while the chapel is an example of a Puritan place of worship with a pulpit where the altar is normally found.

> *Opening times:* Saturday, Sunday and Bank Holiday afternoons from April to June, and weekday and weekend afternoons from July to September.
> *Telephone:* Hungerford 2170.

The old Elizabethan manor house known as Littlecote is the ironically pleasant setting for a ghastly crime which took place there in 1575, and a subsequent haunting. Its details are known because of a statement a Great Shefford midwife, Mrs Barnes, made to a magistrate, Mr Anthony Bridges, on her deathbed. She related that one night a stranger rode up to her house in the village and told her that her services were required immediately by a lady of quality. Hinting that she would be paid well for her trouble, he said that the confinement must remain a secret, and therefore she would be blindfolded. He mounted his horse and, with Mrs Barnes on a pillion saddle, set off, travelling for about an hour and often going across country.

At length the midwife heard the sound of the horse's hooves on the cobblestones of a courtyard, and here she was lifted down and taken into a long dark passage where the blindfold was removed.

The stranger led her up to a chamber where she saw a masked woman in labour lying in a bed. She did not recognise the lady, but, as her professional services were required immediately, she dismissed the strangeness of the situation from her mind.

When the child was born the man seized it from her arms and, despite a shrieked entreaty from the exhausted mother, threw it into the fire where he held it down in the coals with the heel of his riding boot until it was dead. With great presence of mind Mrs Barnes, perhaps realising that at a future date there would be an enquiry into the infanticide, cut a small piece of material from a bed curtain with her scissors. As she was led blindfolded down the stairs from the hateful chamber, she counted the number of steps. It was a large sum of money which kept her silent until she knew she was dying and felt the need to bring about some retribution to the murderer.

After her confession suspicion fell on William Darrell – known locally as Wild Will – of Littlecote Manor. Tradition has it that when the investigation took place a hole was found in the bed hangings into which fitted the piece of material which Mrs Barnes had snipped away. The trial of Darrell was held under Sir John Popham who acquitted him, though rumours were rife that he had been bribed to do so. Certainly it is known that William Darrell made over Littlecote to Sir John in 1586 though he continued to live there until his death.

One flaw in this account is that Sir John Popham was not a judge at the time, though he was Attorney-General and it would have been possible for him to have influenced the acquittal. He did become Lord Chief Justice in 1592, and is remembered in history for presiding over the trial of Guy Fawkes. He took possession of Littlecote in 1589 when William Darrell was flung from his horse when riding past a gate which is still known as Darrell's Stile, and which is still haunted by his phantom.

Melodramatic legend asserts that it was the sudden appearance of a child surrounded by flames which caused the horse to shy.

For generations speculation has been rife as to the identity of the unfortunate mother who saw her child immolated. William Darrell earned his nickname through his amorous exploits, and there are several women who would have fitted the role including Ada Darrell, his own sister. One suggestion is that she was the wife of Sir Henry Knyvett, another that she was a Miss Bonham. A letter was found at Longleat towards the end of the last century, dated 2 January 1578, in which Sir John Thynne wrote to Mr Bonham, then staying at Longleat, asking him 'to enquire of his sister touching her usage at Will Darrell's, the birth of her children, how many there were and what became of them; for that the report of the murder of one of them was increasing foully, and would touch Will Darrell to the quick'.

Whoever the tragic mother was, her phantom has returned frequently to the birth chamber. Some of those who have seen it described her as holding an infant in her arms. Other manifestations going back to that terrible night include mysterious bloodstains which appeared on the floor, footsteps made by some invisible person and the echo of agonised shrieking.

In 1927 Sir Edward Wills saw the ghost of a fair-haired woman clothed in what appeared to be a pink nightdress. She was in the passage which led to the Long Gallery and disappeared into a room where his brother slept undisturbed.

LONGLEAT HOUSE
(Map reference: 57)

The house, standing four miles south-west of Warminster, is the home of the sixth Marquess of Bath and is one of the most popular open houses in the country. Its boast is that it offers something for everybody, every day of the year, and earlier on the novelty of its famous lions of Longleat did a lot to entice visitors. Even without such attractions, Longleat is still a remarkable place. The house, which stands in a magnificent park, began as a small medieval priory which was rebuilt when Sir John Thynne acquired it in 1540 and little of its appearance has changed since his time.

Inside, most of the rooms were redecorated in an Italian style and only the Great Hall retains its old appearance. For the stately home enthusiast there is a profusion of rich furnishings, tapestry, paintings and books, and the formal garden outside the house is the work of Capability Brown and Humphrey Repton.

Opening times: Daily, excepting for Christmas Day, all the year round. The Safari Park is open daily from March to October.
Telephone: Maiden Bradley 551.

Of all the phantoms who visit Britain's stately homes, the best known is the beautiful apparition which returns to the Green Lady's Walk at Longleat. Perhaps this is because her story was the great scandal of her day or more likely because she was such a beauty – a fact borne out by her portrait hanging in the dining-room. The artist depicted her in a gorgeous green gown which is obviously responsible for her being known today as the Green Lady.

Her name was Lady Louisa Carteret, daughter of the Earl of Granville, and her mistake was to become the second wife of Thomas Thynne, second Viscount of Weymouth, in the reign of Queen Anne. The unsuitability of the marriage caused much comment in aristocratic circles, and Sarah Jennings, the formidable Duchess of Marlborough, expressed publicly her astonishment that someone as charming and beautiful as Lady Louisa should have married such an unpopular man.

The viscount, whose son was to become the first Marquess of Bath, had inherited Longleat but chose not to spend much time there, preferring to live in a small manor house in nearby Horningsham. His aversion to grand residences was regarded as yet another example of his eccentricity, and to this was added the general opinion that he was a strange and even vicious man. His first marriage had been a very unhappy one and soon the gossips were delighting in the fact that his second was heading in the same direction.

At Longleat the high-spirited Lady Louisa refused to accept this state of affairs. Having recognised that she had made a mistake in her choice of a husband, she found solace in the arms of a romantic young lover. So she could spend as much time as possible in his company, she brought him secretly into Longleat where he stayed hidden on the top floor of the house.

The couple thought that the hours they spent together in the maze of rooms and passages up there were secret and safe, but some slip on the part of Lady Louisa must have aroused the suspicions of her husband. One day he quietly followed her up the stairs and surprised her greeting a stranger in a corridor. The viscount drew his sword and Lady Louisa watched as her husband and lover fought a merciless duel up and down the passage.

Finally the viscount ran his sword into the gallant who had cuckolded him and, according to legend, had his body secretly buried in the cellar. Then, as though Longleat held a great repugnance for him, he moved back to Horningsham where he spent the rest of his life. After her death the ghost of Lady Louisa was seen in the corridor where she had watched her lover die, and thus it became known as the Green Lady's Walk. She is said to move up and down it as though distracted by terrible grief.

It is a romantic if unhappy story which was given confirmation by a startling discovery two and a half centuries after it had taken place. When central heating was being installed in Longleat it was necessary for the engineers to have the cellar floor excavated in order to connect the system into the boiler room. Beneath the ancient flagstones was found the body of a young man. As the air reached it, it began to dissolve into dust and soon all that remained were his high Queen Anne-style leather boots.

For the next Longleat ghost we must go from the Green Lady's Walk to the Red Library where the benign shade of Sir John Thynne returns to the surroundings he created and loved. After the Dissolution he purchased the Augustinian priory which had stood on the Longleat site for over two-and-a-half centuries. The price he paid was just over fifty pounds, but he spent a fortune on building the present Longleat after the original building which he was renovating burned down in 1567.

The new house, with its hundred rooms, was conceived in the Italian style then so popular in England. Sir John spared nothing to make it a masterpiece, though in life he never saw it in the form he had planned as he died in 1580 before its completion. Such was his love for Longleat that it is easy to understand why he should return to it in the form of an old gentleman in a black robe who appears to be one of the most welcome phantom visitors to a British stately home.

Another haunting which takes place at the top of the house is also connected with a library – Bishop Ken's Library which is revisited at midnight by the good bishop himself on the anniversaries of his death in 1711. As with Sir John Thynne he is a gentle ghost who remains drawn to the surroundings he loved. For twenty years this library was his refuge from the world and here he wrote his *Divine Poems* and many hymns.

Bishop Ken was one of those men who could only act in accordance with what his conscience told him was correct even if it was in conflict with his personal interest. This unyielding trait became apparent when he would not allow Nell Gwynne to lodge in the close of Winchester Cathedral despite enormous pressure from the court and his own well-wishers. Had he taken this stand over the mistress of any monarch other than Charles II things would have gone ill for him, but the easy-going king did not make an issue of it though the incident remained stored in his keen memory. Later when he was told that a new bishop needed to be appointed for Bath and Wells, he asked, 'Where is that good little man who refused his lodging to poor Nell?'

In 1688 the bishop's principles in refusing to publish James II's 'Declaration of Indulgence' landed him in the Tower with six of his peers. England at that time feared 'Popery' as the fires of Smithfield were still close enough to terrify the public and the seven bishops were acquitted. Bishop Ken shared this antipathy to Roman Catholicism, yet when Protestant William and Mary came to the throne he refused to take the oath to them on the grounds that he had already done so to James II. For this stubborn thinking he lost his bishopric and things would have gone sadly for him had not the then Viscount Weymouth offered him a refuge for life at Longleat. Here he spent most of his time working in the Old Library which was later given his name.

Longleat's lesser known supernatural manifestations include a spectre which haunts the Noble Courtyard, one which materialises in a linen cupboard and something which raps on the door of a bedroom. Of more interest is the tradition which states that doom will fall on house and family if ever the swans of Longleat fly away. Some of these birds have acted as harbingers of disaster, rather as white birds were supposed to presage ill tidings for the House of Hapsburg.

In 1916 the wife of the fifth Marquess of Bath was looking out of a window when she saw five swans flying low towards the house. They circled it, beating their wings close to her window before one suddenly changed course and flew towards the horizon while the remaining four returned to the lake.

The marchioness likened the swans to members of her family and took the departure of the lone swan as an omen that her eldest son, Viscount Weymouth, had been killed on the Western Front. The next day her fear was confirmed by a War Office telegram.

On another occasion this psychic lady looked up at the roof and asked why workmen were up there, and why there were dust sheets shrouding the furniture in the hall. Her family were bewildered – there were no men on the roof. But her words were recalled when it was damaged by fire and work had to be carried out as she described.

That there is still psychic activity at Longleat was something I discovered when I visited the house in the course of writing this book. Before I was shown the Green Lady's Walk and Bishop Ken's Library, I happened to mention that in using dowsing rods I found I could get a 'fix' on sites associated with the paranormal.

It was suggested that as an experiment I should roam the passages at the top of the house – which I never visited before – and see if I could tell which passage, and what part of it, was the scene of the duel and Lady Louise's haunting.

Holding the copper rod in the approved style, I walked along several corridors until at one spot the rods suddenly came together and remained touching while I walked about twenty feet where they sprang apart. This, I was told, was exactly the haunted area. In Bishop Ken's Library the rods indicated which alcove was the one for his manifestations and finally in a passage below the ground floor, the rods crossed at the spot where I was afterwards told the bones of Lady Louise had been found.

While the mechanics of dowsing are not yet fully understood, the fact that the rods reacted to what might be termed as psychic vibrations so accurately indicates that Longleats' ghosts are something far more definite than old traditional tales.

OLD WARDOUR CASTLE
(Map reference: 83)

The remains of Wardour Old Castle are to be found in Wardour Park off the A30 between Shaftesbury and Salisbury. It was the home of the Arundell family until the Civil War when it was partly destroyed. Later the Arundells built a fine Palladian House nearby which is also open to the public and which has beautiful rooms with interesting plasterwork and eighteenth century paintings and sculpture.

Opening times: Department of Enviroment standard hours.

It is the spectre of Lady Blanche Arundell which materialises at Wardour Castle. She goes back to the castle's most stirring time when Lord Arundell went to fight for the king during the Civil War, leaving his wife Blanche to hold the castle with a handful of retainers.

In May 1643 a force of 1300 Roundheads besieged it and for five days Lady Blanche held out with her twenty-five defenders. Food and shot soon ran out, but not until two mines were exploded under the walls were the gates opened in surrender.

Wardour became a Parliamentarian garrison but after Lord Arundell died his successor returned to Wardour with a small force and recaptured it. From then on the family lived in the undamaged corn store until a new castle was built over a century later.

The family died out nearly forty years ago, but the ghostly Lady Blanche has since been glimpsed as dusk gathers about the walls where she loaded the match-lock guns of the defenders during the historic siege.

Another supernatural aspect of Wardour was the belief that white owls appeared to the family as a sign that the death of the head of the household was close at hand.

Yorkshire

HAWORTH PARSONAGE
(Map reference: 45)

Providing a local industry for Haworth village in West Yorkshire, the old parsonage was once the home of the extraordinarily talented and tragic Brontës. The appearance of the house conveys the sadness of their lives as it gazes blankly over the crowded graveyard of the church where the Reverend Brontë once preached, and where Charlotte, Emily and Bramwell Brontë are buried.

Under the care of the Brontë Society, the rooms of the parsonage have been returned to their original appearance and fascinating relics of the family are displayed.

> *Opening times:* Apart from being closed for the last three weeks in December, this literary memorial is open on weekdays all the year round and on Sunday afternoons.
> *Telephone:* Haworth 42323.

To me the most fascinating literary shrine is the Haworth Parsonage which is a Mecca for Brontë-addicts from the world over. Here to be seen among the fascinating relics of this extraordinary family are the minuscule books which were the product of childish imaginations heightened by physical isolation and spiritual claustrophobia. This claustrophobia is still conveyed by the old grey building overlooking the graveyard despite the tens of thousands who walk through it each year. And I always come away marvelling how so much genius could have resulted from such an unlikely background.

More evocative is a ruined house high up on the moor known as Top Withins – the house which Emily Brontë used as the mould for Wuthering Heights. When the weather permitted the children delighted in escaping from the parsonage and their eccentric father, and trekking over the moorland. Emily must have sat and gazed at Top Withins and peopled it with Heathcliff, Cathy and the rest. The most reserved of the sisters, her outlet for her secret emotions was in the passions of her characters.

It is no wonder that her ghost has been seen in the locale which meant so much to her. She appears as a slender figure with her head bowed in thought wandering on the path which runs from the parsonage to her beloved moors. Sometimes her appearances are in the early afternoon, on other occasions in the gloaming.

NEWBURGH PRIORY
(Map reference: 66)

Near Coxfold, seven miles south-east of Thirsk in North Yorkshire, is Newburgh Priory which was originally established by the Augustinians in the 12th century. Anthony Bellasis, the chaplain to Henry VIII, purchased the priory in 1529 and transformed it into a mansion. The final result of the additions made to the priory gives an interesting mixture of Tudor, Jacobean and 18th-century architectural styles.

The priory has many historical associations and today visitors are shown the tomb of Oliver Cromwell. No one can be absolutely certain that it contains the Protector's remains but it is quite possible, as his third daughter Mary was married to Viscount Fauconberg who owned Newburgh from 1647 to 1700.

Of particular attraction to visitors is the wild water garden, the collection of rare alpine plants and the glorious rhododendrons in the grounds.

Opening times: Wednesday afternoons from 1 July to 26 August.
Telephone: Coxwold 435.

In his book *Secret Britain* G. B. Wood claims that 'for eeriness, and a sense of the past breaking its way into the present, few places can hold a candle to Newburgh Priory'. This eeriness seems to be the result of a curse laid by the prior when the establishment became a victim of the Dissolution in 1539. When the order for closure came builders were at work on a new room in the upper storey of the building. Outraged that the whim of a mortal king could abolish God's church which had been all-powerful for centuries, the prior sought a way of laying a curse on those who should benefit from the priory's confiscation, and the unfinished chamber gave him the answer.

He swore that if in the future any secular owner was to complete the work on the room his family would suffer an unexpected death. For nearly four hundred years the curse was respected and the room remained just as it was on the day the Augustinians were forced to leave their home.

By the beginning of the 20th century superstition had waned and ancient curses had become relegated to quaint old folktales. To Sir George Wombwell it seemed ridiculous that the apartment should not be put to good use, and he brought in plasterers to finish off the work which had been interrupted so long ago.

Almost immediately news came that the South African War had claimed the life of the Wombwell heir – and the work was instantly halted before further catastrophe could befall the family.

Another strange relic from the Dissolution is a casket attached firmly to the mantelpiece of one of the bedrooms. The story goes that one of the monks placed a missal in it with the instruction that after he and his fellows had gone it must never be moved from that spot. Not long ago a servant removed the missal and took it to her own bedroom, whereupon she immediately fell ill and remained so until the book was replaced in its box which, to prevent any further trouble, has been kept locked ever since.

Apart from such ominous legacies, Newburgh has its ghosts. A male phantom wearing a wig and tight breeches has been glimpsed emerging from the unfinished room. The present owner of the priory has been quoted as saying, 'I have seen some evil things in my time, but nothing so vile as the look on that fellow's face!'

More bizarre is the ghost of a murdered woman whom tradition claims kicks her severed head down a flight of stairs.

TEMPLE NEWSAM HOUSE
(Map reference: 80)

This large Jacobean house is surrounded by a huge park five miles east of Leeds, and walking through it one still finds a hint of its bygone historical associations. The estate was owned by that amazing medieval organisation, the Knights Templar, which was finally suppressed on the excuse of heresy and witchcraft. The

Templars' leader was burnt at the stake in Paris and their vast fortunes channelled into greedy royal coffers.

The estate passed to the D'Arcy family who held it until 1537 and then into the ownership of Sir Arthur Ingram. His additions gave the house its final shape, though more rebuilding and redecoration was carried out at the end of the 18th and 19th centuries.

Temple Newsam was the birthplace of Lord Darnley, the consort of Mary Queen of Scots, and during Elizabeth's reign it was a centre of English and Scottish political intrigue. It was finally inherited by the late Lord Halifax who in 1922 sold it to Leeds Corporation.

In its Georgian rooms there are splendid collections of silver, ceramics, paintings and furniture.

Opening times: Tuesdays to Sundays all the year round, also open on Bank Holiday Mondays.
Telephone: Leeds 647321.

Lord Halifax – the author of the well-known *Lord Halifax's Ghost Book* – frequently stayed at his sister's home of Temple Newsam where he saw a ghost in the Blue Damask Room at three o'clock one morning. He described the gliding apparition as an elderly lady of great beauty wearing a lace shawl over her shoulders, and said, 'She paused at a dressing-table, searched for something and then passed into the Miss Ingram room.'

Other supernatural manifestations at the house include the sound of an invisible person sighing and a noise 'as of furniture being moved' which has alarmed people who spent the night in a certain room beneath the Long Gallery.

IRELAND

CASTLE MATRIX
(Map reference: 18)

Standing at Rathkeale on the main Killarney road in County Limerick, Castle Matrix goes back to the mid-15th century when it was built by the seventh Earl of Desmond. Today it has on display authentic furnishings, *objets d'art* and historic documents and is the headquarters of the Irish International Arts Centre. It is noted for its spit-roasted medieval gourmet banquets which are provided for groups by arrangement.

> *Opening times:* Saturday, Sunday, Monday and Tuesday afternoons from June to 2 September.
> *Telephone:* Rathkeale 139.

Castle Matrix has a spiritual as well as a supernatural tradition which originated in the wellspring of Celtic culture. Seán O'Driscoll, who has lovingly restored it to its present state, told me, 'The history of Castle Matrix has an aura of mysticism which goes back more than five centuries before the Christian era. The fortress of Matres (the castle's original name) is sited upon a sacred pagan rock, the Celtic sanctuary to Matres, Mother of all their gods and the triple goddess of Love, Fertility, and Poetry. Poetry in this instance was related to magic and prophecies. The Matres site was the centre of the Celtic Oracles.

'In 1440, James Fitzgerald, the seventh Earl of Desmond, constructed his residential fortress Castle Matres (later anglicised to Matrix) directly upon the Celtic site of that name. Like his father, Gerald, he was skilled in poetic lore and was known as a "rhymer". His more-renowned father, Gerald the Poet, gained a reputation as a magician from his mystical research. The earliest recorded Norman-Irish verse came from the pens of these earls.

'The native writers describe Earl Gerald as "a lord of marvellous bounty and mirth, cheerful in conversation, charitable in his deeds, easy of access, a witty and generous composer of Gaelic poetry, a learned and profound chronicler, and one of the foreign nobles that held the learning of Erin and its professors in

149

greatest reverence". The earl still lives in Irish legends, according to which he did not die but walked under the waters of nearby Lough Gur, from which he emerges every seven years to visit his estates.'

The story of the castle continued peacefully until 1487 when a murder was committed in the Great Hall. The victim was James, the ninth earl and grandson of the man who had built the castle, and the details of the crime are hazy. It is generally believed that the earl's brother encouraged the castle servants to kill him, but if the instigator of the deed hoped to gain the castle by his plotting, his ambitions were cut short by the executioner.

The castle's happier tradition of poetry reaching back into pagan times has continued through the centuries, an example of this occurring in 1580 when two little-known young men (each twenty-eight years of age) met for the first time at Castle Matrix and began their lifelong friendship – Edmund Spenser had yet to have a poem published in his name, and volunteer Captain Walter Raleigh was yet to come to the queen's attention. A few years after, the two men ranked among the most renowned poets of the Elizabethan Age. In 1500, both had roles in the suppression of the Desmond rebellion. Spenser was employed in London as Secretary to the Viceroy, Lord Grey; and Raleigh was one of eight Captains under Grey's command.

By 1583, the fifteenth Earl of Desmond was killed and all his territory confiscated. Soon after, Castle Matrix was granted to a transplanted English family, the Southwells. Although Protestant favourites of Elizabeth, this family had one son who became a Jesuit priest and was destined to be hanged, drawn and quartered at Tyburn. Curiously enough, the Jesuit Robert Southwell ranks (like Raleigh) among the leading Metaphysical Poets in the English language.

Seán O'Driscoll says that since the castle's restoration several supernatural happenings have been reported, most of which have been attributed to the Magician Earl or to the murdered ninth earl. What is perhaps of more interest are the visions people have experienced while staying at Matrix which many believe are induced by the fact that the site was dedicated originally to the Celtic goddess. Apparently these visions are prophetic in nature, but those who have experienced them are reluctant to go into detail – it is as though they do not wish to devalue the experience by turning it into a topic for conversation.

MALAHIDE CASTLE
(Map reference: 60)

'In the midst of urban development stands Malahide Castle, a 250-acre oasis, the contours of which have changed little in 800 years,' says the Castle's brochure. And it is no exaggeration, Malahide is a splendid example of a house beautifully preserved and steeped in Anglo-Irish history.

The original Anglo-Norman building was rebuilt long ago, and today the oldest part of the house is the keep-like tower dating from the 14th century. The addition which followed it was the Great Hall from the reign of Edward IV who bestowed upon the incumbent lord and his heir the grand title of Admiral of Malahide and Seas Adjoining. This hall is the only essentially medieval hall still in use in Ireland.

The house is packed with treasures from the past – Flemish panels, fine examples of pre- and post-Restoration furniture, hand-painted leather wall-hangings and a collection of portraits regarded as the most complete record of any one family still remaining in Ireland.

> *Opening times:* All day Monday to Friday from January to end of December, and Saturday, Sunday and Bank Holiday afternoons November to end of March, after which Saturdays open in the late morning until the end of October.
> *Telephone:* 452655.

With its beamed ceiling, walls of family portraits and gleaming period furniture, the Great Hall of Malahide makes a perfect setting for the appearances of the castle's two phantoms. The first of these – the White Lady – is one of the most intriguing to grace a stately home despite the fact that nothing appears to be known about her except for a painting showing her in a flowing white dress hung in the hall for many years. What makes her unique is that it has been recorded that, from time to time, she would suddenly become three-dimensional (if a ghost can be thought of as having dimensions) and step out of the frame in order to glide about the castle's rooms.

The other ghost was last sighted in 1976 when the castle was taken over by two Irish tourist organisations after the death of Lord Talbot de Malahide which broke a family connection with the castle going back 791 years. The ghost who appeared then is known as Puck, the Caretaker of Malahide Castle. During his life in medieval times his responsibility was to keep watch from a turret which is known today as Puck's Staircase. He never failed in his job as watchman, but for some forgotten, or unknown, reason he hanged himself in the castle.

He has been seen on many occasions, being quite unmistakable as he was only four feet high. His appearances were mentioned in letters of the Talbot family as far back as the 18th century.

One of the treasures of Malahide is a beautiful Flemish carving of the Coronation of the Virgin which is mounted above the fireplace in the Oak Room. It depicts the Virgin Mary surrounded by four angels, two of which are in the act of lowering a crown upon her head. Tradition gives this sculpture a miraculous quality around the time of the Civil War which etched such deep scars on Ireland.

Miles Corbet of Norfolk, one of the regicides who signed the death warrant of Charles I, was sent by Cromwell in 1650 to administer the affairs of Ireland. When he took up residence at Malahide Castle it was widely believed that the figure of the Virgin vanished from the carving as though in protest, the place where it had been remaining blank for twelve years. In 1659 Corbet was arrested in Dublin but escaped abroad and it was only after he had been recaptured and executed in London in 1661 that the image of Mary returned to the carving.

Another story connected with the castle refers to Maud Plunkett – maid, wife and widow in one day! It seems odd that there is no ghostly echo from her tragedy, especially as her tomb lies within the precincts of the ruined Abbey of Malahide beside the castle. Before her death in 1440, Maud was married in the abbey to the son of Lord Galtrim, yet before the day was out her new husband and her father, the Baron of Killeen, were summoned to take part in a battle. The same evening the corpse of the bridegroom was carried home and the story became the theme of Gerald Griffin's ballad *Bridal of Malahide*.

SPRINGHILL
(Map reference: 79)

Standing on the Moneymore–Coagh road a mile from Moneymore in County Londonderry is Springhill, a splendid 17th-century manor house with white roughcast walls and a slate roof. In the care of The National Trust, it has been described by Lyn Gallagher, the Trust's information officer for Northern Ireland, as 'our most celebrated haunted house'.

Of interest to the visitor is Springhill's renowned oak staircase, collections of furniture and paintings, a cottar's kitchen and a costume museum. Outside there are unusual barns with carved gables flanking the front of the house.

Opening times: Afternoons daily, excluding Fridays, from 1 April to 30 September. Also open on Good Friday.

At Springhill paranormal activity centres on the broad oak staircase and in a certain upstairs bedroom. Although the phenomena continue today, vivid reports of them go back over the years. Just a century ago a house guest named Miss Wilson sat up very late one night chatting with Milly Conyngham, the daughter of the house, in the Cedar Room.

After Milly had finally bade her friend good night and retired upstairs to her room, Miss Wilson noticed that she had left her diary behind. Fully aware of the anxiety which the loss of this repository of secrets would cause the owner, the kindhearted guest left the room to take it up to her. Outside the Cedar Room she paused to admire the dramatic effect of moonlight pouring down the great staircase, and then to her surprise she saw the tall figure of a woman appear at the top of the stairs. The apparition moved on to the door of a bedroom, paused and threw up her hands in despair and then faded away.

The experience filled Miss Wilson with fear, and the questioning of members of the household the next morning did not make her feel any better. All swore they had been in bed and asleep at that hour.

Later another lady house guest – a Miss Hamilton – was given the bedroom at the door of which Miss Wilson's ghost had vanished. That night she had an alarming experience which she related to Charlotte Lenox-Conyngham who was so impressed that she wrote down the account as follows:

'I had gone to bed in the great four-poster, the fire had died down and I had begun to grow drowsy, when it suddenly seemed as if the room was filled with excited people – servants, I thought – who were pushing, and wrangling in whispers. I felt overcome by fear, but just then I heard a clicking sound behind me, as though a door had been opened, and then a light shone at my back, and someone seemed to come out through this light and stilled the commotion, so that all fear left me, and after a while I fell asleep. It was strange that I fancied a door had opened behind me, as the head of the bed is against the wall where there is no door.'

At this point Charlotte had interrupted her, saying, 'But there *is* a door behind the bed though quite hidden by the tester of the bed, and it has been papered over for quite a long time.'

Years later the lady of the house had the bed removed and the wallpaper stripped off in order to see beyond the hidden door. She found that it opened into a powder closet which had a bricked-up fireplace and window. On the dusty floor lay an ancient pair of gloves and a small pouch containing bullets.

The psychic disturbances are thought to have been triggered by the death of George Lenox-Conyngham who, like his one-time friend Lord Castlereagh, took his own life. His wife Olivia wrote the following in the family Bible:

'George Lenox-Conyngham being in a very melancholy state of mind for many months prior, put an end to his existence by a pistol shot. He lingered from the 20th of Nov. 1816 to the 22nd, and died, thanks to the Almighty God, a truly penitent Christian. He was in the 64th year of his age. Buried at Lissan.'

The room in which he committed suicide is the upstairs bedroom, and later on another member of the family, Una Lenox-Conyngham, wrote '. . . that upstairs room has been the centre in after years of some curious experiences (could they be called "after effects"?) which seem to confirm the theory that any strong outburst of anguish lingers for a long period in the place where it led to a tragic happening, and under special conditions, causes some persons to see a vision of the event and of those who took part in it. There are strange stories of this room . . . the Hon. Andrew Stuart, husband of George's eldest daughter, when sleeping here used to find that his belongings were mysteriously moved in the night. Two small great-great grandsons of George, who were in the large four-post bed, were heard by their governess, who occupied the adjoining dressing room, to be talking of a strange lady whom they saw standing by the fireplace. "She must be a ghost!" said one of the children calmly, and without fear.'

While this gives no indication as to the identity of the female ghost, it could be that she was someone who was deeply affected by the tragedy which is suggested by the way she has been seen throwing her arms up in anguish outside the door.

SCOTLAND

ABBOTSFORD HOUSE
(Map reference: 1)

Situated just south of the A72 three miles west of Melrose, the house is of great interest to admirers of Sir Walter Scott. It was his concept, a re-creation of the old Scottish halls which he described with such detail in his novels, and which today houses his collection of historical relics as well as personal mementoes.

Opening times: Weekdays from 23 March to 31 October, and on Sunday afternoons during that period.

Abbotsford House was built as a labour of love in the early part of last century by Sir Walter Scott. It was his dream – perhaps to be expected from such a romantic writer of historical novels – to build himself a baronial home complete with crenellations. The building of Abbotsford began in 1817 and took eight years to complete. Within the first year of construction Sir Walter became aware of supernatural activity which he described as a 'violent noise, like the drawing of heavy boards along the new part of the house'.

This phenomenon occurred at two o'clock in the morning and was repeated the following night at the same time. It awoke Sir Walter who, seizing an antique broadsword, set off to investigate, but although he searched thoroughly where the sounds appeared to emanate he could find no natural explanation. Strangely, when the mysterious noises reached their height the man in charge of the building died suddenly, after which Sir Walter was left in peace.

The work was completed in 1825 but Scott had little time to enjoy it. Through no fault of his own financial disaster struck him the following year, his creditors taking over his estate. For Scott there was only one way to regain Abbotsford, and that was by writing his way out of trouble. If ever an author burned the midnight oil it was Scott as novel after novel flowed from his exhausted pen.

In 1830 his debts had been cleared with honour and Abbotsford was his again, but the tremendous creative effort it had needed had been too much for him and he died the same year. His death took place in the Abbotsford dining-room where he had asked to be brought so he could spend his last hours looking out at the Tweed which flowed nearby.

On several occasions a silent ghost has been glimpsed in the dining-room, which does not seem at all unusual when one thinks of the bond which the novelist had with his home.

BEDLAY CASTLE
(Map reference: 8)

Situated at Chryston, Glasgow, at the junction of the A81 and the A727, Bedlay is a fine example of a typical old Scottish castle, and houses a fine collection of antiques.

Opening times: Normal hours.

According to a book published in 1880 a clergyman was called to exorcise the ghost of Bedlay Castle who was described as 'a big man'. The ceremony may have been effective for a while but within the last decade the ghost has reappeared at the castle along with the sound of phantom footsteps.

The apparition is said to go back over six centuries when, in 1350, a bishop who resided at Bedlay died in a lake there in what can only be described as 'sinister circumstances'.

CRATHES CASTLE
(Map reference: 26)

Situated on the A93 three miles east of Banchory, Crathes is one of Scotland's best examples of an early Jacobean castle. It dates from 1553 and today it is known for its Great Hall and early painted ceilings. It is in the care of The National Trust for Scotland

Opening times: Weekdays, and Sunday afternoons, from 1 May to 30 September.
Telephone: Crathes 525.

The Green Lady's Room is where the sad ghost of Crathes Castle has frequently been seen crossing the floor to a fireplace whose mantelpiece is supported by vaguely sinister figures. When she reaches this, the Green Lady stoops and lifts an equally ghostly infant from the hearth.

The fact that this re-enactment was connected with a past tragedy was proved when renovations were being carried out some years ago and workmen found the skeletons of a young woman and a baby secreted beneath the fireplace.

A legend of Crathes tells that in the 17th century a daughter of the castle became pregnant by one of her father's ghillies. Terrified of the disgrace should the news get abroad, the family kept the girl isolated until her confinement. Then it was decided that the only way to remove the threat of scandal completely was to arrange for her murder. Such a solution is not so far-fetched as it seems at first when one remembers that today there are societies where transgression of certain moral codes automatically results in execution.

Often it seems the discovery of a victim's remains lays his or her ghost, but in the case of the Green Lady her manifestations have continued as strong as ever.

CULZEAN CASTLE
(Map reference: 27)

Said to be one of the finest examples of an Adam house in Scotland, the castle is perched on the edge of a cliff off the A719, twelve miles south-west of Ayr. It was Robert Adam who rebuilt it towards the end of the 18th century. Culzean's claim to fame this century is that President Eisenhower used an apartment there on several occasions. Today the castle is in the care of The National Trust for Scotland.

Opening times: Daily from 1 April to the end of October.
Telephone: Kirkoswald 269.

The supernatural manifestations which occur at Culzean Castle have one of the most painful origins of any haunted site in Britain. It goes back to 1570 when one Allan Stewart, Commendator of

Crossragruel Abbey, was made prisoner by Gilbert Kennedy, the fourth Earl of Cassillis, who was determined to increase his domains by the inclusion of the abbey land.

Allan Stewart was taken to Culzean and told that all he had to do to obtain his freedom was to sign a document which would transfer the abbey lands to Kennedy ownership. As was to be expected no Stewart would accept such an offer from a Kennedy, and the earl issued orders to his henchmen to try more direct methods of coercion. The captive was taken down to the Black Vault where a great fire had been lit, his clothes were torn off him and he was tied to a spit. Slowly he was turned in front of the fire as though he was an ox being roasted whole. To complete the analogy his torturers kept larding him to ensure that he did not burn and find escape in unconsciousness or death.

Compared to the torment of the Black Vault the ownership of the abbey lands became unimportant and before long Stewart cried out that he would sign. The spit stopped revolving, the chains were released and the prisoner was dragged to where his enemy waited with a parchment ready for his name. When he had obtained the transfer, the earl decided to keep Stewart a prisoner at Culzean until he was certain that the land was actually his, and no doubt he congratulated himself on his foresight when he found that he needed his captive to sign a confirmatory paper. But Stewart had spent the time brooding on his treatment and he decided he would rather die than see the land pass into Kennedy hands.

Once more he was dragged down to the Black Vault, again he was chained like a side of beef to the spit and rubbed with fat while the fire leapt up in its chimney.

Allan Stewart held out as long as possible, but when human nerves could stand no more and his body revolted against his will he screamed his agreement between charred lips. He was taken down, sluiced with water and forced to endorse the transfer with his trembling signature.

The Priory Council found this real estate transaction rather questionable even by the rough standards of the 16th century. A fine of £2000 was imposed on the Earl of Cassillis and in addition he was forced to pay his victim a pension for the rest of his life – but he kept the lands of Crossragruel Abbey.

Since then some psychic echo of the happening in the Black

Vault has been reported at Culzean. On certain Sunday mornings the roar of the fire and the shrieks of Allan Stewart have sounded again in the castle, the cries becoming more and more feeble until a merciful silence descends.

An interesting aspect of the haunting is that it is an aural re-enactment of an evil event but one which was not terminated by a death.

It is not only the human roasting which has stamped a paranormal impression on Culzean: within the past ten years there have been independent sightings of a misty figure in a passage below the castle. And on certain windy nights there comes the sound of wild bagpipe music which is attributed to the phantom Kennedy Piper.

Strangely enough, there is also a natural curiosity close to the castle which has been known since the advent of the motorcar as the Electric Brae. It is a hill which, when you are driving down it, gives an extraordinary impression that you are ascending.

DUNTRUNE CASTLE
(Map reference: 30)

This 12th-century Scottish baronial castle is situated on the B8025 near Lochgilphead in Argyllshire. Built to guard the surrounding countryside against sea raiders, its origins are shrouded in mystery. In the 16th century a house was incorporated within its ramparts and until 1729 it was held by the Campbells of Duntrune.

Visiting only by written appointment.

A century ago the ancient kitchen slabs of Duntrune Castle were taken up and the men employed on restoration work beheld a skull grinning up at them. When the full skeleton was removed for Christian interment by the Dean of Argyll, it was found that the finger bones were missing. This curious discovery gave proof to the legend of the Phantom Piper of Duntrune.

The story goes back to 1615 when feuding between the Campbells and MacDonalds was at its height. Coll Ciotach, of the MacDonald clan, had captured the castle and garrisoned it with his followers before sailing south to the Isle of Islay.

While he was away the Campbells of Duntrune, who had been masters of the castle for five centuries, counter-attacked and retook the fortress, killing every MacDonald except Coll Ciotach's piper. In those days pipers were regarded as privileged persons, like heralds.

The piper knew that when his master returned he would run straight into an ambush at the castle and somehow he must find a way of warning him that the castle was in the hands of his foes. To this end he composed a special pibroch which to this day is known as *The Piper's Warning to his Master*.

From then on he remained at the highest point of the castle, his eyes roving anxiously over the water in the hope of being the first to pick out the MacDonald boat. At last he saw it and began to play.

The eerie tune floated over the sound, and in his galley Coll Ciotach realised that this was no ordinary welcome. There was something wild and urgent about the melody . . . something that hinted of danger. He ordered his sailors to heave to while he squinted at the castle and the piper silhouetted against the sky.

Apart from that tiny figure Duntrune seemed deserted. Where were his clansmen who should have been coming down to the shore to greet their leader? The more Coll puzzled about it, and the more he listened to the sad wail of the pipes, the more suspicious he became. He shouted a command to his helmsman, the vessel turned and sped away.

At the castle the Campbells, realising the loyal piper had robbed them of their prey, cut off his fingers in savage revenge. He soon died from loss of blood and was buried beneath the flagstones of the castle kitchen, but since then his warning pibroch has been heard again and again skirling from the battlements.

DUNVEGAN CASTLE
(Map reference: 31)

The castle at the head of Loch Dunvegan on the Isle of Skye is known to Scots around the world as the home of the MacLeod of MacLeod. It dates back to the 13th century and until the Fairy Bridge was built across a moat-like ravine it was only possible to enter it from the sea through a portcullis-guarded opening in the rocks.

Among the treasures to be seen at the castle today are the drinking horn of a 12th-century chieftain Rory More, mementoes of Bonnie Prince Charlie, and letters relating to visits to Dunvegan by Dr Johnson and Sir Walter Scott. Most important of all is the Fairy Flag of Dunvegan.

Opening times: Daily excluding Sundays from 18 May to 1 October, afternoons only from 6 April to 16 May and 3 October to 29 October.

Dunvegan Castle is the Mecca for members of the MacLeod clan from the world over, and in the realm of folklore it is famous for its association with a fairy rather than a ghost. To reach this remote castle you have to cross the ancient Fairy Bridge which has a strong supernatural reputation. It used to be claimed that no horse could be ridden or led across it without it plunging out of control because of invisible influences.

According to the legend of Dunvegan one of the members of the MacLeod clan, who owned the castle, married a fairy woman. The couple were perfectly happy until the husband became an old man while his wife remained like a young girl – fairies do not age as fast as humans. At last the time came for her to return to her own folk and she said a sad farewell to her mortal husband at the Fairy Bridge.

Here she gave him a final present – a flag which could bestow up to three wishes. To obtain a wish a member of the clan merely had to wave it, and twice it has been waved to summon supernatural help. The first time was in 1490 at the Battle of Glendale and the second in 1580 at Trumpan. On both occasions the MacLeods were granted victory. There is one wish left, and I wonder if it will ever be invoked.

As well as being able to bring aid to the clan when it was desperately needed, the flag is said to draw shoals of herrings into Dunvegan Loch when it is unfurled. It was also hung above the bridal bed of members of the MacLeod family in order to ensure a fruitful marriage. If you should visit the castle you can see this rare fairy relic on display in the Fairy Room in the 16th-century South Tower.

GLAMIS CASTLE
(Map reference: 37)

Situated off the A94, five miles west of Forfar in Tayside, Glamis goes back to the 14th century when Robert II of Scotland granted the lands of Glamis to the Earls of Strathmore who have held it ever since. It was the childhood home of Queen Elizabeth, the Queen Mother, and the birthplace of Princess Margaret. Of special interest are its collections of fine furnishings, armour and paintings. In the grounds there is a remarkable sundial with eighty-four dials.

> *Opening times:* Afternoons, excluding Saturdays, from May to 1 October. Also Easter weekend afternoons.

Without doubt the world's most famous haunted residence is Glamis, Scotland's oldest inhabited castle. Apart from a fascinating company of ghosts it has a dark mystery going back through the centuries which, if it were fiction, would be regarded as the archetypal Gothic horror story. Added to this is a touch of royalty. Here it was that Malcolm II was assassinated in 1034. Seven years later Macbeth, the Thane of Glamis, stabbed Duncan to death in the gloomy hall which still bears his name, and where for generations the stain of his blue blood remained a mute testimony to this celebrated regicide.

Because of the castle's supernatural and historical associations I feel there is no need to apologise for dealing with it at length, so let us begin with the tradition of the Sealed Room. It has been a subject of speculation for so long that people outside the initiated members of the Strathmore family have attempted to solve the riddle, but always in vain. For example, in the 1880s house guests decided, while their host was away in Edinburgh, to try and find the secret chamber. As the castle has over a hundred rooms this was no easy task, but they ingeniously hung towels out of the window of every room it was possible to enter. It is said that they did see a window without a towel, but were unable to locate the room to which it belonged because their investigations were halted by the unexpected return of the earl who was enraged at the unauthorised search.

Various authors have been intrigued by the tradition. Augustus Hare, in *The Story of My Life*, wrote: 'In the depth of the wall is another chamber more ghastly still (he had been describing Duncan's Hall) with a secret transmitted from the fourteenth century, which is always known to three persons. When one of the triumvirate dies, the successors are compelled by a terrible oath to elect a successor. Every succeeding Lady Strathmore, Fatima-like, has spent her time in tapping at walls, taking up boards and otherwise attempting to discover the secret chamber, but all have failed.'

Writing about Glamis, Sir Walter Scott said: 'It contains also a curious monument of the peril of feudal times, being a secret chamber, the entrance of which, by the law or custom of the family, must only be known to three persons at once, viz. the Earl of Strathmore, his heir apparent, and any third person whom they may take into their confidence.'

There have been many guesses as to the reason for the hidden room, a widespread suggestion being that it was a cell for some sort of monster. On 28 October 1966 the *Daily Telegraph* published an article which made this reference to such a creature: 'The walls in the old castle are immensely thick – up to fifteen feet in places. Somewhere in them lies the secret of Glamis – a mysterious chamber where a previous Earl is supposed to have kept hidden a hideous monster, a son born half man, half beast.

'For 150 years the monster lived in the castle, only emerging to crawl about at night . . . One historical fact adds support to the legend. A portrait in the drawing-room shows the 1st Earl with his sons: two boys and a peculiar little dwarf.'

There is a rumour in circulation that the imprisoned monster died in 1921, so the length of time it must have survived brings in a paranormal element.

Another theory is that a long time ago a servant was found to be a vampire and was locked in the secret room where he remained in a state of catalepsy, his ancient flesh uncorrupted and his unnatural thirst waiting to be satisfied with the unsealing of his crypt.

A different explanation is suggested by the Victorian ghostlorist the Reverend F. G. Lee who wrote: 'There is no doubt about the reality of the noises at Glamis Castle. On one occasion, some years ago, the head of the family, with several companions, was determined to investigate the cause. One night, when the disturbance was greater and more violent than usual, and it should be premised strange, weird and unearthly sounds had often been heard, and by many persons, some quite unacquainted with the ill repute of the Castle, his lordship went to the Haunted Room, opened the door with a key, and dropped back in a dead swoon into the arms of his companions; nor could he ever be induced to open his lips on the subject afterwards.'

What caused his lordship to faint when he investigated the mysterious sounds? Tradition says that the knocking goes back to the time of a bitter feud between the Ogilvies and Lindsays. After a clan battle, a party of defeated Ogilvies straggled into Glamis demanding sanctuary. The lord of the castle had no wish to arouse the anger of the fugitives by refusing them, on the other hand he feared the wrath of the Lindsays if he gave shelter to their enemies. He therefore led the Ogilvies to a remote chamber and once the unsuspecting clansmen were inside, slammed the heavy door, turned the key and left them hammering in despair on the massive woodwork.

It has been suggested that when Lord Strathmore forced open the ancient door he saw the mound of the prisoners' skeletons, some of which still had the bones of their arms clamped in their teeth as starvation had driven them to eat their own flesh.

Yet another explanation goes back to Alexander, the fourth Earl of Crawford, nicknamed in his day 'Earl Beardie'. In *The Picture of Scotland*, published in 1827, Robert Chambers wrote: 'It is the tradition of Glamis that he (Earl Beardie) was playing at cards in the Castle, when, being warned to desist, as he was losing, he swore, in a transport of fury, that he would play till the day of judgement. On this the Devil appeared in the company, and they, room and all, disappeared.'

There may be a grain of truth which inspired this story as a gambling scandal once occurred at Glamis. *All the Year Round* gave this account: 'The old feud between Lindsays and Lyons had so far healed over that the members of the two families dined, and drank, and diced together, like fine old Scottish gentlemen as they were. According to local tradition, the play one night at Glamis was very high, and when its owner had lost all his money, he staked his estates, one after the other, against the victorious player. At last Glamis itself was set on the turn of a card – and lost. Then the head of the house, maddened by his losses, accused his guest of cheating. The reply was a blow, swords were drawn, and after a few passes the victorious guest ran Lord Strathmore through the body, and thus sacrificed all his winnings.'

How does this melodrama tie in with the forbidden room? According to local folklore it was the scene of a card game between the Devil and one of the lords of Glamis known by his retainers as Earl Patie. Notorious for all forms of dissipation, his greatest vice was gambling, and he shocked his puritanical neighbours by playing at cards and dice on Sundays, ignoring the class structure when it came to games of chance. He would be friendly with the meanest castle servant when he was desperate for a gambling partner.

One stormy Sunday night in a long ago winter the earl strode restlessly about his hall. Because of the Scottish attitude to the Lord's Day, he had not been able to raise a hunting party and now he was dangerously bored. Ordering a deck of cards, he looked about for partners. The ladies of Glamis were at evensong, the servants remained out of sight afraid their master would force them to profane the Sabbath. He even tried to bully a priest into taking a hand, and received a sermon in reply – so 'swearing tremendously' and declaring he would be happy to play with the Devil himself, he took the pack and retired to a chamber in the old tower.

As one expects from such tales, it was not long before a deep voice demanded if the earl wanted a game. The earl retorted that he did and a dark stranger, wrapped in a black cloak, limped in and picked up the cards. The earl must have felt a pang of fear at the appearance of his mysterious partner – especially after his rash declaration – but the gambling madness was upon him and soon he forgot his doubts.

Finally the stranger suggested a stake so high the earl was forced to admit that he did not have the cash to match it – but, he added, if he lost he would put his name to any bond the stranger might draw up.

He lost, and when he died five years later he must have discovered the nature of the hellish contract he had signed. Long afterwards supernatural sounds – echoes from that satanic card game – tormented the castle inhabitants. At length the room in which the malady lingered was locked and the passage leading to it blocked by a wall of masonry.

Mrs Maglagan, wife of the Archbishop of York, related how,

after the death of her brother-in-law Lord Strathmore in 1865, his heir was initiated into the family secret by the lawyer and the agent of the estate, after which he went to his wife and said, 'My dearest, you know how often we have joked over the secret room and the family mystery. I have been into the room; I have heard the secret; and if you wish to please me you will *never* mention the subject to me again.'

She also described how the new earl set about improving the castle, one of his schemes being the construction of a staircase from a lower hall – known as the crypt – to the chapel. While the family were away in London one of the workmen accidentally found an ancient door which looked as though it had not been used for many years. Filled with curiosity he set about opening it and began to walk down a long passage but after a few steps he became scared and retreated, telling the clerk of works of his discovery.

'Immediately all the work was stopped and the head man telegraphed to Claude in London and to Mr Dundas, the lawyer, in Edinburgh,' wrote Mrs Maglagan. 'Both arrived by the earliest possible train and subjected the workman to a severe examination as to what he had or had not seen, the end of it being that he and his family were subsidised and induced to emigrate.'

One cannot leave the mystery of the hidden room of Glamis without this comment, reported to have been made by the fifteenth Earl, the great-grandfather of the Queen: 'If you could only guess the nature of the secret, you would go down on your knees and thank God it was not yours.'

Glamis Castle abounds in conventional ghosts – a White Lady has been seen to glide along the avenue leading to the castle, another spectre is a very tall, spindly figure known as 'Jack the Runner', while a little black servant – believed to have been the victim of ill-treatment – has materialised by the door of the sitting room used by the Queen Mother.

The Reverend Lee told this story of a phantom warrior: 'A lady and her child were staying for a few days at the Castle. The child was asleep in an adjoining dressing-room, and the lady, having gone to bed, lay awake for a while. Suddenly a cold blast stole into the room, extinguishing the nightlight by her bedside, but not affecting the one in the dressing-room beyond, in which her child had its cot. By that light she saw a tall mailed figure pass into the dressing-room in which she was lying. Immediately thereafter there was a shriek from the child. Her maternal instinct was aroused. She rushed into the dressing-room and found the child in an agony of fear. It described what it had seen as a giant who had come and leant over its face.'

Mrs Maglagan also recounted an extraordinary dream coincidence. As Lord Strathmore's sister-in-law, she was a frequent visitor to the castle, but her dream actually occurred at Tullyallan Castle on the night of 28 September 1869. After retiring she dreamed she was at Glamis watching some horses in the park when the dinner gong sounded. She walked towards the Blue Room, where she slept on her visits, to change her clothes but in the corridor she met a housemaid holding pieces of rusted iron.

'Where did you find those?' she asked the girl.

The maid explained that she had been cleaning the grate in the Blue Room when she noticed a stone slab with a ring set in it. She managed to raise the stone, and in a hollow beneath it found the fragments of metal.

'I'll take them down with me,' Mrs Maglagan said. 'His lordship likes to see everything that is found in the castle.'

Then, in her own words, 'As I opened the door of the Blue Room the thought crossed my mind: "They say the ghost always appears if anything is found. I wonder if he will come to me." I went in and there, seated in an armchair by the fire, I saw a huge figure of a man with a very long beard and an enormous stomach, which rose and fell with his breathing. I shook all over with terror, but walked to the fireplace and sat down on the coalbox staring at the ghost. Although he was breathing heavily I saw clearly that it was the face of a dead man.'

Still in her dream, Mrs Maglagan found the silence unendurable. To break the tension she held up the pieces of iron, saying, 'Look what I have found.'

The spectre sighed.

'Yes, you have lifted a great weight off me,' he said. 'Those irons have been weighing me down ever since . . .'

'Ever since when?' asked the Bishop's wife.

'Ever since 1486.'

'At that moment, to my great relief, I heard a knock at the door,' Mrs Maglagan wrote. 'It was Caroline (the maid) opening my shutters, and the sun was streaming cheerfully into the room. I sat up in bed and found that my nightgown was quite wet with perspiration. I came downstairs very full of my dream, and still more of the fact, as I believed, that although the room was in all other respects exactly like the one I thought I remembered so well, the fireplace was in a different corner. So persuaded was I of that that next year I saw the room at Glamis and found that my dream memory was right and my waking memory wrong, I could scarcely believe my eyes.'

Two years later Mrs Wingfield, a daughter of Lord Castledown, met Mrs Maglagan's brother Eric. When she heard about his sister's experience she told him of an extraordinary coincidence. While Mrs Maglagan had been staying at Tullyallan, Mrs Wingfield was a guest at Glamis, and on the same night Mrs Maglagan had her dream, she had dreamed too.

She was occupying the Blue Room and went to bed as usual. Before going to sleep she read by the glow of her nightlight, and after dozing off she suddenly awoke with the sensation that she was not alone in the room. She sat up and saw, seated before the fire, a 'huge old man with a long flowing beard'. He turned and gazed at her and she realised that although he appeared to be breathing, 'the face was that of a dead man . . .'

Records of Glamis begin in 1372 when King Robert II gave it to his son-in-law Sir John Lyon who brought with him an heirloom in the form of a cup believed to be associated with the destiny of his family. The removal of this talisman from its original home was held responsible for the sinister things which happened after its arrival at the castle.

No doubt its influence was blamed in 1383 when Sir John Lyon, then the Great Chamberlain of Scotland, was slain in a duel. The family's misfortunes came to a climax in 1537 when Janet Douglas, widow of the sixth Lord of Glamis, was arrested for practising witchcraft. William Lyon accused her of using Black Magic in an attempt to kill James V of Scotland, also accusing her son and her second husband, Archibald Campbell, who fell to a merciful death while attempting to escape from Edinburgh Castle.

Lady Janet's fate was far more terrible. Chained to a stake on Castle Hill she was burned as a witch, though – according to an old chronicle – she met her fate 'with great commiseration of the people, being in the prime of the years, of a singular beauty, and suffering all, though a woman, with a manlike courage'. It is her ghost which has been seen, surrounded by a halo of fire, above the Glamis clock tower.

Young Lord Glamis was more fortunate. Although sentenced to death with his mother, the court suspended the sentence until he should reach his twenty-first birthday, by which time the malicious William Lyon, who had laid the charges against the family, made a death-bed confession that he had acted out of spite and there was not a shred of truth in his evidence. The prisoner was released and his estates were restored to him.

The strange knocking which from time to time reverberated through part of the castle has been attributed to the hammering which accompanied the building of Lady Janet's scaffold.

An account of this ghostly echo appeared in *All the Year Round* in 1880. The contributor, after prefacing it with an assurance to readers that he had it on good authority, wrote: 'A lady, very well known in London society, an artistic and social celebrity, wealthy beyond all doubts of the future, and what is called a very cultivated and instructed, but clear-headed, and perhaps slightly matter-of-fact woman, went to stay at Glamis Castle for the first time. She was allotted very handsome apartments, just on the point of junction between the new buildings – perhaps a hundred or two hundred years old – and the very ancient part of the castle. The rooms were handsomely furnished; no gaunt carvings grinned from the walls; no grim tapestry swung to and fro, making strange figures look still stranger by the flickering firelight; all was smooth, cosy, and modern, and the guest retired to bed without a thought of the mysteries of Glamis.

'In the morning she appeared at the breakfast-table quite cheerful and self-possessed. To the inquiry how she had slept, she replied: "Well, thanks, very well, up to four o'clock in the morning. But your Scottish carpenters seem to come to work very early. I suppose they put up their scaffolding quickly, though, for they are quiet now." This speech produced a dead silence, and the speaker saw with astonishment that the faces of members of the family were very pale.

'She was asked, as she valued the friendship of all there, never to speak to them on that subject again; there had been no carpenters at Glamis Castle for months past. This fact, whatever it may be worth, is absolutely established, so far as the testimony of a single witness can establish anything. The lady was awakened by a loud knocking and hammering, as if somebody were putting up a scaffold, and the noise did not alarm her in the least. On the contrary, she took it for an accident, due to the presumed matutinal habits of the people. She knew, of course, that there were stories about Glamis, but had not the remotest idea that the hammering she had heard was connected with any story.'

A curious story connected with Glamis was published in *Ghostly Visitors* in 1882, and the fact that it had no satisfactory dénouement added rather than detracted from it.

In this case it was a doctor of medicine who was staying at Glamis in 1878. Just before dinner he was looking from his window when a man walked in and asked him to come immediately as one of the guests, by the name of Miss Seymour, had been taken ill.

'In the parlour,' the doctor wrote, 'to which I followed him, I found a lady lying in an armchair apparently in a dead faint. I instantly adopted the usual remedies, and she was rapidly recovering her consciousness, when the strange gentleman exclaimed with a sneer, "Is that the way in which you doctors treat your patients? I will show you how I cure them"; and before I could prevent him he had stabbed her in the breast with a dagger. Then both vanished.'

The effect on the doctor can be imagined. Fearing he was the victim of hallucination, he knelt on the floor to see if there were any traces of blood but there was nothing. He then went into the dining-room to see if Miss Seymour was among the guests assembling there – and sure enough she entered as though nothing unusual had happened. There was no sign of the man with the knife.

Two years passed, during which the doctor often reflected on the strange drama he had seen played out. Then at a ball in Gloucester he met the young lady again and she explained that she was no longer Miss Seymour as she had married since her visit to Scotland.

'My husband is here, somewhere,' she said. 'I must find him and introduce him to you.'

As you may have guessed the husband was the image of the phantom the doctor had seen stab Miss Seymour. Making an effort to control his excitement, the doctor said: 'Then your husband – your fiancé then – was with you at Glamis?'

· 'Oh, no, he wasn't,' she answered. 'He has never been to Glamis.'

And there the story ended – or did it?

There is no shortage of other ghostly incidents connected with the castle, but let us look at just one more example which was described by Augustus Hare. The author was staying at the castle when one night a fellow guest looked out of his window to see a black coach drive up to the castle – without the normal scrunch of gravel – and pull up below him. A minute passed, then the driver looked up and, flicking the backs of his black horses with the reins, drove away. The guest was impressed by his 'marked and terrible face'.

At breakfast the next morning he remarked to Lord Strathmore, 'You had a very late arrival last night.'

At his account of the sinister coachman the earl went pale and answered in a low voice that no one had arrived at the castle.

Some weeks later the same man was staying in Paris on the third floor of a hotel. One day he rang for the lift, and when it arrived and the gates opened he jumped back in shocked surprise – the lift operator appeared identical to the mysterious coachman. Seeing the guest hesitate, the operator impatiently clashed the gates together. An instant later a cable snapped and the cage hurtled down the well. All its occupants were killed in the impact.

INVERARAY CASTLE
(Map reference: 50)

For five centuries this castle, at Inveraray in the Strathclyde region, has been the home of the Dukes of Argyll and the headquarters of the Clan Campbell. The present house was built round an earlier square tower towards the end of the 18th century by Roger Morris and Robert Mylne. Visitors can see the state rooms, the armoury and the Great Hall and examples of 18th-century furniture, excellent paintings and tapestries.

Opening times: Weekday mornings and afternoons, excluding Fridays, and Sunday afternoons from the first Saturday in April until the end of September.
Telephone: Inveraray 2203.

At first sight of Inveraray Castle you could not be blamed if, for a second, you wondered whether you really were in Scotland or the Valley of the Loire. With towers capped by conoid roofs of gleaming slates, it looks exactly like a French château. This dates back to the mid-18th century when the castle was redesigned as an example of the neo-Gothic revival, giving a façade to the older part of the castle which goes back a further two and a half centuries. Its unusual greenish stonework imparts a mystic charm, as though it had materialised from some fairy realm into a suitably exotic setting.

Prior to the deaths of one of these chiefs, ravens were wont to wheel in unusual numbers about the castle, but a more dramatic portent was described by Mr H. W. Hill, one-time secretary of the English Church Union, in *Lord Halifax's Ghost Book*.

He recalled that in 1913 he dined with Niall Campbell just after the death of his father Lord Archibald Campbell. During the meal the subject of omens came up, Mr Hill mentioning that the ominous gathering of ravens had been described in the Scottish Press. Niall Campbell said he believed in the authenticity of the tradition and added that a much more mysterious sign was the galley which sailed over Loch Fyne just prior to his father's death. This vessel, shaped like the ship which is part of the Campbell arms, had three silent figures standing on board as it sailed up the loch and then continued its voyage overland to vanish at a spot associated with St Columba, which had been given to the Church by the Campbells.

It was believed the galley always made this journey when the head of the clan was dying, and on the recent occasion of Lord Archibald's death it had been seen by many witnesses. Not all had the Celtic blood which is often a requirement for the 'second sight' for recognising such portents; an Englishman seeing the galley sail over the shore of the loch shouted: 'Look at that funny airship!'

Apart from the 'ominous birds of yore' and the galley, Inveraray Castle is haunted by a phantom harper who was executed by order of the Marquis of Montrose when he drove Lord Argyll from his castle in 1644. The ghost, which has been described as 'a harmless little old thing', appears in Campbell tartan. Apart from his harping, he makes a noise in the Green Library as though books are being flung about, though when anyone goes to investigate the disturbance every volume is in place.

Inveraray was also the scene of an extraordinary phenomenon on 10 July 1758, when the famous physician Sir William Hart was walking in the grounds of the castle accompanied by a friend and a servant. One of the men looked up into the sky and gave an exclamation of amazement. The other two looked up and saw a battle taking place above them. Many of the visionary soldiers wore the uniform of the Highlanders, and they were desperately attacking a fort defended by a French garrison.

The dumbfounded watchers saw the soldiers endeavour to scale the ramparts again and again, while the defenders poured volleys of musket fire on them. The British force seemed to be without scaling ladders and the men climbed on each other's shoulders in almost suicidal attempts to gain the top of the fort's walls. Finally they withdrew, leaving the ground covered with their dead comrades. As the musket smoke ceased to roll from the French stronghold the scene of carnage dissolved.

Soon afterwards two ladies, the Misses Campbell of Ederin, arrived at Inveraray breathless with a tale they had to tell. They had been on the road which ran between Kilmalieu when they saw a vision of a battle in the sky. They described exactly the same spectacle as the three men had seen.

There was great speculation as to what it could mean. At that time England was at war with the French in America, and it was known that the Highlanders were stationed at Albany, but the exact nature of the battle was not known until weeks later when an official bulletin stated that the Highlanders had been in action against a French fort at Ticonderoga on Lake George and over three hundred men were killed and as many wounded. The date of the battle was 10 July – the same date that the five people had seen its 'mirage' in the sky above the castle. When it was seen that the name of Duncan Campbell was on the list of those killed in action a curious story was remembered.

Duncan was the master of Inverawe House which is situated some miles north of Inveraray Castle. Two years before he died, Campbell was walking on a hillside near his home. He saw a man racing towards him over the heather, and when he came close he saw that he was drenched with blood.

'Save me,' he gasped. 'The avengers of blood are on' my track.'

Taking pity on the fugitive, Duncan swore that he would shelter him 'by the word of an Inverawe which never failed friend or foe yet'. He led him to a secret cave which was known only to the lairds of Inverawe, for in those troubled times such hiding places were often necessary for survival. It had the advantage of a fresh water spring in it, and tradition has it that Robert the Bruce once hid there.

Having promised the man that he would return with some food when it was dark, Duncan returned to his house to find an excited messenger waiting for him.

'Your foster brother Donald has been murdered by a man called Macniven,' he cried. 'We have tracked the murderer close to this place. I have come to warn you in case he should ask for your protection.'

Duncan went deathly white. The messenger, knowing the affection he felt for Donald, thought that it was the effect of grief.

When night fell Duncan went to the cave with food as he had promised. Now the pity he had felt for the fugitive had turned to hatred, but he had given his word as an Inverawe to shelter him, and he was bound by his promise.

Back at Inverawe House he went to bed but he was unable to sleep. Suddenly he was aware of a presence in the room, and he looked up to see the ghostly form of his foster brother gazing down at him. His clothes were torn and bloodstained, and his face was a ghastly hue. At last he spoke with great difficulty.

'Shield not the murderer,' he said. 'Blood must follow blood.'

Despite Donald's words, Duncan carried food to Macniven the next day, and that night the ghost appeared again and repeated his demand. But Campbell could not forget that he had given his word and therefore could not avenge his foster brother, though the next morning he told Macniven: 'I can help you no longer, you must escape as best you can.'

That night the ghost of Donald appeared for the third time, and declared: 'I have warned you once, I have warned you twice – it is too late now. We shall meet again at Ticonderoga.' He did not return after that.

At that time Duncan was mystified by the name Ticonderoga. He had never heard it before, and it was not until he was in America two years later with his regiment that he was to realise that the Indian name for the French position they were attacking was Ticonderoga, though his brother officers – to whom he had confided the story – had tried to keep the indigenous name of the fort a secret from him.

As he lay dying, Duncan Campbell looked up at his general and muttered his last words: 'You deceived me. This is Ticonderoga . . . for I have seen him.'

WALES

CASTELL COCH
(Map reference: 17)

Close to the village of Tongwynlais, six miles north of Cardiff, Castell Coch is a romantic pseudo-Gothic building which was restored from the 13th-century castle of Ifor Bach by the Marquis of Bute in the Victorian era. It is now in the care of the Welsh Office.

Opening times: **Open daily the year round (Sunday afternoons only) except for Christmas Eve, Christmas Day, Boxing Day and New Year's Day.**

Although the present castle is just over a hundred years old, it has inherited a phantom from the old castle on whose foundations it was built. The ghost is that of a cavalier said to be searching for a golden hoard. Local tradition asserts that such a treasure was hidden in a large subterranean chamber centuries ago by the warrior Ifor Bach. There is a hint of the Round Table in such a tale because as well as a treasure there is a sleeping army of Ifor's men waiting to be reanimated on his return, a legend similar to several Arthurian traditions of a sleeping host in different parts of the country.

The tale adds that the treasure is guarded by three terrible eagles who tear to shreds men foolish enough to enter the mysterious vault. A knight who thought he'd outwit them by wearing armour which had been given a holy blessing still met the same fate. Perhaps the phantom cavalier lost his life in a search for gold to help finance the royalist cause.

It is perhaps just a quaint old tale, on the other hand there might just be a treasure down there which inspired such stories long ago. After all, Heinrich Schliemann found the ruins of Troy from clues in Homer's *Iliad* which until then had been regarded as an ancient work of imagination.

POWIS CASTLE
(Map reference: 68)

Standing on the outskirts of Welshpool, the castle is a medieval building of red limestone which was strategically sited on a high ridge. As the seat of the Powis family it has been occupied continuously for the last five centuries. Of interest to visitors is its fine interior plasterwork and murals, and collections of paintings, tapestry and furniture. Outside there are the famous terraced gardens which were laid out by the Earl of Rockford in the early part of the 18th century, and which contain fascinating topiary work. The castle is now in the care of The National Trust.

> *Opening times:* Wednesday and Sunday afternoons and Bank Holiday Mondays from 18 April to 27 September. The garden is open on afternoons daily from 2 July to 6 September.

Two hundred years ago Powis Castle was the scene of a cruel trick played on a simple spinning woman who – thanks to the appearance of a ghost – had the last laugh.

In 1780 there was a lot of gossip in Welshpool about a woman who had seen the castle's famed ghost, which was supposed to have revealed a secret to her. John Hampson, a man held in high regard as a preacher by the Wesleyan Methodists, was curious about the rumours, and he interviewed the woman who vowed that the story was true and that there were many witnesses who would vouch for her story.

She explained to Mr Hampson that she was a spinster in both meanings of the word; she was unmarried, and she had earned her living by spinning. As farmers in the district grew their own flax she went to their farmhouses where she spun it on the spot. On one occasion, when her usual customers had no work for her, she decided to try her luck at the Red Castle.

When she arrived at the gloomy fortress she was told by the steward that the Earl of Powis and his family were away in London, and he could not say if a spinner was required. But the wife of the steward, who seemed to have had a cruel streak in her nature, found the woman some sewing work, saying she could stay at the castle and earn her keep until the earl returned. What surprised and delighted the spinner was the luxurious room she was allotted. She had never seen anything so grand in her life and could hardly believe a person as humble as she should be allowed to sleep there. What she did not know was that it was the castle's haunted room, and the steward's wife, encouraged by the rest of the servants, had placed her there to see what would happen.

The servants made up a good fire and left a lighted candle on the table. In one corner was a great four-poster bed so comfortable that the poor spinner could hardly believe such comfort existed. After the servants bade her good night she may have wondered why the lock on her door was turned, but perhaps she thought this was the usual practice in great castles, a safeguard so that strangers like her could not be tempted to take some of the family silver.

Certainly she was not alarmed by this curious custom, and she spent a lot of time looking about her unaware that she was the object of the servants' experiment. Having examined the room, she sat down at the table and in the candlelight read her Bible. Like so many religious-minded people of her time it was her practice to read a chapter before going to sleep. In the yellow light she spelt out the words close to the fire which spread a warm, comforting glow about her.

After a while she looked up and she saw that a man had entered, wearing a 'gold-lace suit and hat'. She was rather surprised, but again everything was so new to her that at first she was not afraid, thinking that perhaps he was some superior type of butler who had come to make sure everything was all right.

The figure walked across the room to a corner window then turned and stood sideways to her, giving the impression that he expected her to say something. The poor woman was tongue-tied, but after a little time – during which she tried vainly to think of something to say to the impressive visitor – he walked off, closing the door behind him as the servants had done.

The fact that this time there was no sound of a lock grating suddenly made her realise that he had entered without the key being turned, and for the first time she realised he must be a phantom.

Everything fell into place. The splendid room, coupled with the unusual attentions of the servants, made her realise that she was there to be haunted. Only one thing occurred to her and that was to pray. She knelt down by her bedside and joining her hands entreated God to protect her.

While she was doing this the gentleman in the gold lace suit appeared once more, and again it seemed as if he was waiting for her to speak. When she was unable to form any words, he disappeared once again through the locked door. She prayed harder that 'God would strengthen her and not suffer her to be tried beyond what she was able to bear'. Perhaps because of her simple faith she found it possible to speak when the apparition appeared for the third time.

'Pray sir, who are you, and what do you want?'

'Take up the candle and follow me and I shall tell you,' replied the figure.

She rose from her knees, took the candle from the table and followed him out of the room and along a seemingly endless corridor until they reached the door of another room.

In telling the story to the Wesleyan preacher, she said:

'As the room was small, and I believed him to be a spirit, I stopped at the door.

He turned and said, 'Walk in, I will not hurt you.' So I walked in.

He said, 'Observe what I do.' I answered, 'I will.' He stooped and tore up one of the floorboards, and there appeared under it a box with an iron handle in the lid.

He said, 'Do you see that box?'

I said, 'Yes I do.'

Then he stepped to one side of the room and showed me a crevice in the wall, where he said a key was hid that would open it.

He said, 'This box and key must be taken out and sent to the Earl in London. Will you see it done?'

I said, 'I will do my best to get it done.'

He said, 'Do – and I will trouble the house no more.'

He then walked out of the room and left me. I stepped to the room door and set up a shout. The steward and his wife, with other servants, came to me immediately, all clinging together, with lights in their hands. It seems they had all been waiting to see the issue of the interview betwixt me and the apparition.

They asked me, 'What was the matter?' I told them the

story and showed them the box. The steward dared not meddle with it, but his wife had more courage and, with the help of the other servants, tugged it out and found the key.'

The woman said that the chest was heavy, but she did not see it opened and therefore could not say what was in it. The steward and the servants carried it away and, exhausted by her experience and at the same time comforted by the thought that the phantom had meant her no harm, she returned to her four-poster and slept until the cocks crowed in the morning.

The steward dispatched the box to his master in London with a letter describing the curious way it had been found. By return came a letter ordering the steward to tell the spinner that if she wished she could reside for the rest of her life in the castle; or, if she wished to remain in her cottage, she would be well provided for. The woman accepted the latter offer, being grateful to the earl and the ghost. But neither she nor Mr Hampson ever heard an explanation for the apparition or got a hint of what was contained in the hidden chest.

INDEX